A Room with a view

by E.M.Forster

Susan Elkin
with additional material by **Nicola Onyett**

Series Editors:
Nicola Onyett and Luke McBratney

HODDER
EDUCATION

AN HACHETTE UK COMPANY

The publisher would like to thank the following for permission to reproduce copyright material:

Acknowledgments:

E.M. Forster: from A *Room with a View* (Penguin, 2012[1908]), with permission by The Provost and Scholars of Kings College, Cambridge and The Society of Authors as the E. M. Forster Estate; **p.vi: Samuel Hynes:** from *The Edwardian Turn of Mind: The First World War and English culture* (Pimlico, 1992), by permission of the publisher; **pp.33, 51, 52, 74, 77–8: Zadie Smith:** from 'Love, Actually', www.theguardian.com/books/2003/nov/01/classics.zadiesmith (2003). Published by The Guardian, 2003 Copyright (c) Zadie Smith. Reproduced by permission of the authors c/o Rogers, Coleridge & White Ltd., 20 Powis Mews, London, W11 1JN; **p.74: Terry Eagleton:** from *Marxism and Literary Criticism* (University of California Press, 1976), by permission of the publisher.

Photo credits:

p.1 © Kiril Stanchev -123RF; **p.6** © rusty elliott - 123RF; **p.16** © ITV / REX / Shutterstock; **p.25** © Roberto Lo Savio - 123RF; **p.30** © Anthony Baggett - 123RF; **p.42** © Michele Falzone / Alamy Stock Photo; **p.44** © Everett Collection / REX / Shutterstock; **p.49** © ITV / REX / Shutterstock; **p.60** © Moviestore Collection / REX / Shutterstock; **p.65** © Geoff A Howard / Alamy Stock Photo; **p.67** © Pictorial Press Ltd / Alamy Stock Photo; **p.69** © ITV / REX / Shutterstock; **p.70** © Granger, NYC. / Alamy Stock Photo; **p.95** © ITV / REX / Shutterstock

Although every effort has been made to ensure that website addresses are correct at time of going to press, Hodder Education cannot be held responsible for the content of any website mentioned. It is sometimes possible to find a relocated web page by typing in the address of the home page for a website in the URL window of your browser.

Orders: please contact Bookpoint Ltd, 130 Milton Park, Abingdon, Oxon OX14 4SB. Telephone: (44) 01235 827720. Fax: (44) 01235 400454. Lines are open 9.00–17.00, Monday to Saturday, with a 24-hour message answering service. Visit our website at www.hoddereducation.co.uk

© Susan Elkin Ltd 2016

First published in 2016 by

Hodder Education

An Hachette UK Company,

Carmelite House, 50 Victoria Embankment

London EC4Y 0DZ

Impression number	5	4	3	2	1
Year	2020	2019	2018	2017	2016

Cover photo (and throughout) © RKTPHOTO:Rachel K. Turner / Alamy Stock Photo

Typeset by Integra Software Services Pvt. Ltd, Pondicherry, India

Printed in Italy

A catalogue record for this title is available from the British Library

ISBN 9781471853692

Contents

Why read this guide?

The purposes of this A-level Literature Guide are to enable you to organise your thoughts and responses to the text, deepen your understanding of key features and aspects and help you to address the particular requirements of examination questions and coursework tasks in order to obtain the best possible grade. It will also prove useful to those of you writing a coursework piece on the text as it provides a number of summaries, lists, analyses and references to help with the content and construction of the assignment.

Note that teachers and examiners are seeking, above all else, evidence of an *informed personal response to the text*. A guide such as this can help you to understand the text, form your own opinions, and suggest areas to think about, but it cannot replace your own ideas and responses as an informed and autonomous reader.

How to make the most of this guide

You may find it useful to read sections of this guide when you need them, rather than reading it from start to finish. For example, you may find it helpful to read the 'Contexts' section before you start reading the text, or to read the 'Scene summaries and commentaries' section in conjunction with the text – whether to back up your first reading of it at school or college or to help you revise. The sections relating to the Assessment Objectives will be especially useful in the weeks leading up to the exam.

NB: All page and chapter references are to the paperback Penguin English Library edition of *A Room with a View* (2012). Where a publication is given in the 'Taking it further' section on pages 100–1, the author's surname and publication date only are cited after the first full reference.

This guide is designed to help you raise your achievement in your examination response to *A Room with a View.* It is intended for you to use throughout your AS/A-level English literature course. It will help you when you are studying the novel for the first time and also during your revision.

The following features have been used throughout this guide to help you focus your understanding of the novel:

Context

Context boxes give contextual evidence that relates directly to particular aspects of the text.

Build critical skills

Broaden your thinking about the text by answering the questions in the **Build critical skills** boxes. These help you to consider your own opinions in order to develop your skills of criticism and analysis.

CRITICAL VIEW

Critical view boxes highlight a particular critical viewpoint that is relevant to an aspect of the main text. This allows you to develop the higher-level skills needed to come up with your own interpretation of a text.

TASK

Tasks are short and focused. They allow you to engage directly with a particular aspect of the text.

Taking it further ▶

Taking it further boxes suggest and provide further background or illuminating parallels to the text.

Top ten quotation

Top ten quotation

A cross-reference to Top ten quotations (see pages 96–9 of this guide), where each quotation is accompanied by a commentary that shows why it is important.

A Room with a View (1908) is a comic romance set mostly in Florence and Surrey that contrasts the sunny freedom of Italy with chilly suburban England. The young heroine, Lucy Honeychurch, a member of the prosperous upper middle classes, eventually defies her society's restrictive rules and conventions to marry – for love – George Emerson, who is not of her social status. Enduringly popular for over a century, the novel has been handsomely filmed twice in the last 30 years.

The time period in which *A Room with a View* is set, the first decade of the twentieth century, is sometimes referred to as the Edwardian Summer. Queen Victoria had died in January 1901 after a reign of almost 64 years and her son Albert Edward, known as Bertie, came to the throne as King Edward VII. Cosmopolitan, widely travelled and extremely popular, the new king was connected by blood or marriage to so many other reigning monarchs that he was nicknamed 'the Uncle of Europe'. The Edwardian era was in great contrast to the reign of his elderly widowed mother; indeed there was a forward-looking sense of excitement with a new century, new monarch and new ideas. The cultural historian Samuel Hynes perfectly captures most people's rose-tinted view of the age in his fascinating cultural survey *The Edwardian Turn of Mind*, noting how deceptively easy it is to feel nostalgia for 'that leisurely time, when women wore picture hats and did not vote, when the rich were not ashamed to live conspicuously, and the sun never really set on the British flag'. Yet Hynes goes on to remind us that while World War I 'dramatised and speeded the changes from Victorian to modern England, it did not make them'. In fact, he suggests, the Edwardian age is better viewed as a time of transition and modernisation: 'aircraft, radiotelegraphy, psychoanalysis, Post-Impressionism, motion picture palaces, the Labour Party were all Edwardian additions to the English scene' (Hynes, 1992: 5).

Given the century between the text's contexts of production and reception, the temptation to retrospectively romanticise the Edwardian era as a golden age of lost innocence is strong. It's all too easy to see the social, cultural and historical framework within which *A Room with a View* is embedded as a gilded moment frozen in time for those fortunate enough to belong to the upper or middle classes. As we read, we can hardly be unaware that the Honeychurches, the Vyses and the Emersons are enjoying the last years of peace and prosperity before the outbreak of World War I ushers in a period of terrible conflict. But we should be careful not to read the text solely through this revisionist lens, wincing at the horrors that lie ahead for Forster's unsuspecting characters; there is no need to sentimentalise a text that is so often bracingly energetic and modern in its outlook.

In terms of style, Forster is moving away from the type of novel that defined the popular fiction of the Victorian era. A Room with a View is much shorter than those nineteenth-century novels initially published in serial form and/or in three hefty volumes, suggesting that Forster agreed with the novelist Henry James' disparaging view of the typical Victorian blockbusters as 'large, loose, baggy monsters'. Notice though, that the traditional ending for a love story is marriage and Lucy and George's love story – at once so much a part of its time and yet equally timeless – still bears this quintessential hallmark of the genre.

Young Lucy Honeychurch has arrived at a guest house – pension – in Florence, escorted and chaperoned by her older cousin Charlotte. The English-owned pension (as spelt by Forster; in Italian it is spelt 'pensione') is an insular community of middle-class English guests, most of whom speak no Italian and are wary of Italians who represent most of what the visitors seek to repress. Mr Emerson, a retired socialist journalist, and his son George, a railway manager, stand out as being different from the other residents as soon as they offer – without fuss or preamble – to change rooms with Charlotte and Lucy because the latter is disappointed not to have been assigned a room with a scenic view of the city and its river.

▲ The River Arno in Florence

The novel is written in the third person but most of the action is presented from Lucy's point of view as we follow her trying to see and to learn, rather superficially, about the art and history of Florence which is what, as a middle-class young woman, she is expected to do on an earnest tourist trip of this sort. She goes to Santa Croce, one of Florence's most famous churches, for example, where she unexpectedly finds herself alone with the Emersons and we see her being disconcerted by Mr Emerson's straightforward frankness. He would like Lucy and George to be friends and says so. His candour contrasts with the usual superficial inhibitedness of Lucy's social class.

On another occasion Lucy is in the city alone. There she witnesses a street murder of a passionate Italian peasant arguing about a small debt and faints because of the blood, drama and tragedy of the incident. George Emerson (has he followed her there?) carries her bodily away from the scene. They then walk back to the pension together. Forster makes it clear that Lucy is attracted to George in a way she does not understand and denies strongly – even to herself. His candour contrasts with the usual inhibitedness that Lucy and her social class are accustomed to.

During a trip to Fiesole, on the hills immediately outside Florence, with a group from the pension, including Mr Beebe, a clergyman who is about to become rector in Lucy's home parish in Surrey, George kisses Lucy. It happens very quickly and unexpectedly and Lucy barely has time to respond because Charlotte appears and catches a glimpse of the 'assault', as she and Lucy thereafter refer to it. Charlotte confronts George about his behaviour and the two women leave Florence for Rome. Part Two of the novel, which forms about two-thirds of the text, finds Lucy back at home with her mother and brother, Freddy, in Surrey. Several months have passed since the end of Part One. Lucy has since spent time in Rome with a Surrey neighbour, Cecil Vyse and his family. She and Cecil now become engaged and conventionally it seems a suitable match. There is a sense of congeniality between them but notably no passion and Cecil is irritating to Lucy, most other characters (Freddy and Mr Beebe, for instance) and to the reader. He tries to control Lucy and dictate to her what to think. He is also supercilious and intolerant. Soon the party is joined by Lucy's cousin Charlotte.

A series of events, including a deliberate piece of manipulation by Cecil, leads to the Emersons coming to live as tenants of a house near the rectory in Summer Street where the Honeychurches live. Cecil has by chance overheard the Emersons talking in the National Gallery and introduced them to local developer Sir Harry Otway. For Cecil this is a joke and a means of discomposing the people of Summer Street.

Inevitably, as Mr Beebe knows and likes the Emersons, it isn't long before George and Lucy meet. And one evening George 'assaults' Lucy again by kissing her, which, when she's told, alarms Charlotte, the only person who knows what happened in Florence. Lucy herself is both excited and uncomfortable in a way she does not fully understand. She tells Charlotte what has happened partly as a way of trying to work out her own feelings.

Lucy's choice is coming closer. She has to decide whether to opt for congenial, perhaps sometimes tiresome, conventional marriage with the all-controlling Cecil or whether to acknowledge what she is really beginning to feel and allow a relationship based on passion and equality to develop with George. If she chooses the latter, and for a long time she refuses to admit to herself it is an option, she will be going against her upbringing and the prevailing attitude of her own social class.

Two heartfelt speeches bring her, eventually, to a decision. The first is from George (p.173–4) who tells her warmly that the backward-looking Cecil, who wants to tell his wife how to think and be, can never be the man for 'you, of all women'. He also declares that he loves her. That night Lucy breaks off her engagement with Cecil although she insists to herself that she has no intention of turning to George. Instead she decides, when she gets the opportunity, to travel to Greece with a pair of elderly sisters she first met in Florence. She feels, or tries to convince herself that she does, the need to escape from everything which has gone before.

> He (Cecil) could not know that this was the most intimate conversation they had ever had.

Top ten quotation

The second pivotal speech comes from Mr Emerson (pp.212–13). He informs her in his usual gently forthright manner that she has loved George all along and she is wrong to deny it. Later Lucy acknowledges that 'it was as if he had made her see the whole of everything at once'

> You love the boy body and soul, plainly, directly, as he loves you, and no other word expresses it.

Top ten quotation

Forster does not show us Lucy and George coming together and the practical difficulties they face such as persuading Mrs Honeychurch of the rightness of this marriage. Instead he takes us to Florence where they are on honeymoon in the room with a view at the same pension. A year has passed since their first meeting there and together they realise that it was Charlotte, not quite as opposed to romantic love as she seems, who opportunistically engineered the turning-point conversation between Lucy and Mr Emerson back in Surrey.

Thus *A Room with a View*, one of two early Forster novels known together as the Italian romances (see also *Where Angels Fear to Tread*), ends where it began with satisfying symmetry and the action plotted across a single year from spring to spring.

Context

Two novels, *Where Angels Fear to Tread* (1905), and *A Room with a View* (1908), have their roots in Forster's year of travel in Italy with his mother in 1903. Both these 'Italian romances', and a number of early Forster short stories, satirise the repressed attitudes of English people abroad, fearful of anything foreign. In *Where Angels Fear to Tread*, widowed Lilia Herriton falls in love both with Tuscany and with Gino, a much younger Italian. The novel presents Italy as representing everything which is earthy, free and attractive just as *A Room with a View* does.

Target your thinking

- How does Forster develop his plot? (**AO1**)
- How does Forster convey his meaning? (**AO2**)
- How do the events in the novel relate to the context in which Forster was writing? (**AO3**)

Part One

Chapter 1: The Bertolini

Lucy Honeychurch is disappointed on arrival at an English guest house in Florence, the Pension Bertolini, not to have been assigned the promised room with a beautiful view of the River Arno. As she and her chaperone (Forster spells it 'chaperon') and cousin, Charlotte Bartlett, discuss this over dinner, they are overheard by another guest, Mr Emerson, who offers to exchange with them the rooms he and his son George are occupying. Although the prudish Charlotte initially refuses, shocked by Mr Emerson's directness, eventually the rooms are swapped, after the English clergyman Mr Beebe mediates between the ladies and the Emersons.

Context

The role of the chaperone is highly specific. Charlotte is an older relative of Lucy's, so not exactly an employee as a governess would be. Her role is to accompany and supervise her young cousin during her continental tour. Charlotte has been funded by Lucy's mother to take care of her young daughter and she is forever conscious of this fact.

Build critical skills

Closely analyse how Forster establishes the relationship between Lucy and Charlotte at the beginning of the novel.

Taking it further ▶

Read the first chapter of the novel two or three times and then watch the opening of the 1985 film version directed by James Ivory. How successfully do you think the director has transferred Forster's characters and themes from page to screen?

Commentary This opening chapter introduces several key characters. We see childlike Lucy, naïvely enthusiastic – 'I do so always hope that people will be nice' – metaphorically stamping her foot because she has no view of the River Arno and exaggeratedly 'saddened' by the 'Signora's unexpected accent' – that is, the fact that the hotel proprietor is actually a London Cockney. Forster also introduces Lucy's supremely irritating travelling companion, querulous, tiresome Charlotte, who initially refuses Mr Emerson's kind offer to swap rooms because she worries that there's an intimacy in moving into a room immediately vacated by a man. The language Forster uses to describe Charlotte's feelings when Mr Emerson persists in offering to give up his room is telling in its sexualised innuendo: 'Miss Bartlett, though skilled in the delicacies of conversation, was powerless in the presence of brutality.' This can be read as telling us more about Charlotte's own inner longings and repressed sexuality than about any concern she has for Lucy's reputation if they put themselves under any sort of obligation to a socially 'inferior' man such as Mr Emerson.

The male characters are also clearly drawn in this opening scene. The apparently sensible clergyman Mr Beebe acts as a go-between here, as he is to do several times during the course of the novel. The unusual and 'childlike' Mr Emerson speaks the exact truth with no fudging. He doesn't bother with superficial etiquette, which leads Mr Beebe to find him 'rather a peculiar man' who 'will not keep his opinions to himself'. Lucy, however, begins to warm to him, seeing him as a **kind old man** who has enabled her to have what she wants. Forster signals, though, that there is more to young George Emerson than a man who 'hasn't learned to talk yet' because a question mark ('note of interrogation') has been left on the mirror in the larger room which Charlotte has taken. The reader assumes that it was a private message for Lucy whom George would have expected to take the better room.

This opening chapter, like most of the novel, is presented via the omniscient narrator entirely from Lucy's point of view. It is her response to Charlotte's prevarication – 'the sense of larger and unsuspected issues' – and Lucy's 'bewildered' responses (p.13) that Forster stresses here, along with her reaction to Mr Emerson's offer, meeting Mr Beebe and her first impressions of the pension.

> Top ten quotation

Context

```
Forster's presentation of Lucy in this first scene is a
perfect example of the classic 'fish out of water' literary
trope, situating his central protagonist in a totally alien
new situation. Comedy - or, as in Forster's other famous
'Italian romance' Where Angels Fear to Tread, tragedy -
emerges as the English characters either learn to adapt to
their new environment, or fail to. The trope goes back as far
as Aesop's fable of the Town Mouse and the Country Mouse.
```

Taking it further ▶

In George Eliot's Victorian bestseller *Middlemarch* (1872), the heroine Dorothea Brooke and her clergyman husband Edward Casaubon have a disastrous honeymoon in Rome in which Casaubon behaves more like a know-it-all tour guide than a loving husband. You might enjoy comparing Eliot's detailed and evocative descriptions of this ill-matched couple with Forster's presentation of Lucy and George.

▲ The Santa Croce

primogeniture:
the firstborn son
inheriting the lion's
share, as opposed
to an equal division
into parts of an
inheritance.

Context

Built in 1294, the
Basilica di Santa
Croce is Florence's
principal
Franciscan church
and one of the
city's most famous,
beautiful and
historic buildings.
The artist
Michelangelo,
politician
Machiavelli,
scientist Galileo
and composer
Rossini are all
buried in Santa
Croce.

Context

Until World War I changed social attitudes for ever,
respectable, young, unmarried middle-class women would not
generally have been expected to travel, or even to go out,
unescorted. The protection of a girl's 'reputation' – i.e.
her virginity – was the unspoken issue here. Virginity was
crucial to a 'good' marriage in a world which judged male
and female sexual behaviour very differently.

CRITICAL VIEW

A Marxist critic might interpret this premium placed on Lucy's virginity
as symptomatic of a society in which women have a market value. The
need to protect the laws of **primogeniture** and property inheritance
meant that the worst thing that could happen to a man like Cecil Vyse
would be to discover that his wife had been seduced and thus devalued
by another man. Later in the novel (p.152) Lucy observes to herself that
Cecil 'desired her untouched' even though the 'touching' she is worried
about is just a single kiss.

Chapter 2: In Santa Croce with no Baedeker

Lucy is to be escorted during a visit to Santa Croce by Eleanor Lavish, a writer
of popular fiction who is also a guest at the Pension Bertolini. It turns out that
Miss Lavish is an inattentive substitute chaperone for Lucy, as even before they
reach Santa Croce she sees someone else she knows and bounds off, having
confiscated Lucy's trusty Baedeker travel guide. Alone in Santa Croce, Lucy
meets the unconventional Emersons again. They annoy the shallow and snobbish
Reverend Cuthbert Eager, who is acting as an unofficial tour guide to a group of
English visitors, but Lucy is intrigued by the Emerson's unconventional attitudes
and honest, straightforward manner of speaking.

Commentary This chapter opens with Lucy observing from the window
of her room with a view, the bustling everyday life of Florence with its river
men, soldiers, children and street sellers. Forster, like Mr Emerson, clearly
values what he ironically calls 'such trivialities' (p.15) and satirises visitors
whose sole purpose is 'to study the tactile values of Giotto, or the corruption
of the Papacy' by commenting that it is 'as well' that Miss Bartlett, who would
of course value the Giottos far more highly than the street scene, arrives to
disturb Lucy's reveries. Mr Emerson is interested in exploring the culture of
the ordinary Italian people, as opposed to the vast majority of the English visitors
who prefer a sanitised Baedeker-endorsed programme which edits out the real
modern Italy and presents the country as little more than a vast museum and art
gallery.

Context

For centuries, 'Italy' was 'a geographical expression' used to describe the famous boot-shaped peninsula as opposed to a functioning political state. A series of city-states controlled by super-powerful rival families or foreign powers, the country was not unified until the nineteenth century. The crucial political and social movement that consolidated all the different states into the Kingdom of Italy with Rome as the official capital was known as the *Risorgimento* (meaning 'resurgence'). Its iconic leaders and national heroes included the first king of Italy, Victor Emmanuel, the charismatic statesman, Camillo Cavour, and the legendary general, Giuseppe Garibaldi.

Context

Baedeker's *Handbook to Northern Italy* was one of a series of iconic travel guidebooks, the first of their kind. German publisher Karl Baedeker founded the company in 1827 and it lasted until 1948, a reflection on the growth of middle-class European tourism in the nineteenth century and beyond. Forster's point is that English travellers like Lucy are so dependent on the authorised views of Baedeker that they forget to think and look for themselves.

Charlotte Bartlett, so tiresomely and falsely self-deprecating that to modern eyes she may seem typically 'passive-aggressive', clearly doesn't want to go out after breakfast whereas the excited Lucy, quite naturally, does. It is indicative of Charlotte's self-absorbed incompetence that she allows Lucy to set forth with the glamorous and eccentric Eleanor Lavish, who assures her that Lucy will be safe as 'Italians understand' the strict code of conduct that surrounds a young Englishwoman abroad. Miss Lavish teases Charlotte by suggesting that Florence is so safe for an environment for her that even 'Mrs Grundy' would be happy to let Lucy go. In this we see another example of Forster's free-thinking attitude and satirical approach to outdated social conventions, as 'Mrs Grundy' is a shorthand reference for the mind-set of an exceptionally obsessive prig or prude. While the original Mrs Grundy was a minor character in a forgotten eighteenth-century play, in time her name came to personify the tyrannical hold over manners, morals and codes of conduct possessed by the pathologically respectable.

Taking it further ▶

In Charles Dickens' *Little Dorrit* (1857), the upwardly mobile Dorrit family hires a sort of life-coach called Mrs General to provide the social polish that will wipe out all traces of their scandalous past. The prissy catchphrase 'Prunes and Prism' sums up the genteel pretentions Mrs General foists upon the Dorrits, as Dickens questions the pretentious falsity endemic among many members of the middle and upper classes. You might enjoy comparing Dickens' social satire with that of Forster, as poor Amy Dorrit's life is reduced to 'surface and varnish and show without substance'.

With Miss Lavish's departure, Lucy is alone in the basilica without her Baedeker and annoyed at the thought that she will thus be unable to appreciate what she sees without its official guidance. Mr Emerson gently teases her about her attitude – something that he and the avant-garde Miss Lavish – 'short, fidgety, and playful as a kitten, though without a kitten's grace' – would, presumably agree about. The lecturing clergyman, Mr Eager, is annoyed with Mr Emerson for the latter's insightful comment that saying Santa Croce was **'built by faith'** simply means that the workmen weren't paid properly. Mr Eager objects to Mr Emerson's intervention for several reasons: social (he does not have the 'right' class background), political (he is expressing a left-leaning socialist view) and religious (he criticises 'the superstition and ignorance that lead men to hate one another in the name of God'). Mr Emerson continues to disconcert everyone he meets by speaking blunt truths – usually earnestly and politely – in disregard of the genteel English convention dictating that one should only indulge in 'small talk' on uncontroversial matters.

Top ten quotation

Forster presents both Mr Eager and Mr Emerson as teachers in this chapter, but their pedagogies could hardly be more different. Mr Eager pontificates and lectures in an attempt to indoctrinate his biddable pupils, the earnest spinster sisters Miss Teresa and Miss Catharine Alan. Mr Emerson does things very differently. He gently questions Lucy to prompt her to think more independently and move beyond her narrow comfort zone, tells her she doesn't need the textbook (her Baedeker) she is using as an intellectual crutch and tells her that she can learn a lot from interacting with a young person of a similar age who is also thirsty for knowledge – his son George.

The first signs of the destabilising effect George will have on Lucy's equilibrium are clear when she compares her response to him with her reaction to his father:

> Lucy could not get cross. Mr Emerson was an old man, and surely a young girl might humour him. On the other hand, his son was a young man, and she felt that a girl ought to be offended with him, or at all events be offended before him. It was at him that she gazed before replying.

(p.23)

Significantly the narrator has already described George as having 'a hint of the teacher about him', and when Lucy allows him to take her to the Giotto paintings she most wants to see 'She felt like a child in school who had answered a question rightly.' George is presented as a perceptive and sensitive young man clearly used to his kindly and well-meaning father's infinite capacity for offending the Mrs Grundys of the world, assuming 'tranquilly' and rightly that Mr Emerson has been snubbed by Mr Eager for voicing his humanist views so forcefully.

Mr Emerson is shown to be a compassionate and thoughtful man of great generosity. Honest and unpretentious, when he quotes some lines from

A.E. Housman's *A Shropshire Lad* (1896) he uses 'his ordinary voice, so that [Lucy] scarcely realises he was quoting poetry'. The lines that mean so much to Mr Emerson are these:

From far, from eve and morning

And yon, twelve-winded sky,

The stuff of life to knit me

Blew hither; here am I.

(p.28)

These simple words seem to sum up his simple humanist philosophy of life. 'George and I both know this, but why does it distress him?' he tells Lucy. 'We know that we come from the winds, and that we shall return to them; and that all life is perhaps a knot, a tangle, a blemish in the eternal smoothness. But why should this make us unhappy? Let us rather love one another, and work and rejoice. I don't believe in this world-sorrow.' When Lucy's first instinct is to agree – 'Miss Honeychurch assented' – the old man simply and movingly asks her to help him teach George how to look at life this way too: 'Then make my boy think like us. Makes him realise that by the side of the everlasting Why there is a Yes – a transitory Yes, if you like, but a Yes' (p.28). But it is too soon. The meeting in Santa Croce is extremely significant in terms of developing our understanding of the characters of Lucy and the Emersons and showing that at this early stage in her Italian (and emotional) journey, Lucy still has much to learn. She cannot handle Mr Emerson's comment that her getting to know George better would do them both good; simultaneously intrigued and shocked, she retreats into 'matronly' conventionality and makes the comically lame suggestion that if George has a problem he could try collecting stamps, a safe hobby that 'did no end of good' for her brother Freddy. The chapter ends with George spotting Charlotte Bartlett, who has finally turned up, much to Lucy's initial dismay. Mr Emerson's repeated exclamation of 'Poor girl' baffles Lucy, but the reader knows that he is sorry to see her about to be sucked back into the conventional world represented by Charlotte, which is riddled with sham and pretence.

Chapter 3: Music, Violets and the Letter S

Lucy plays the piano in the Pension Bertolini and escapes into Beethoven. Mr Beebe listens to her playing and remembers once hearing her play at Tunbridge Wells in England. The rest of the chapter comprises a conversation between Lucy and Mr Beebe and Miss Catharine Alan who joins them. They discuss Charlotte Bartlett, Miss Lavish and the Emersons.

Commentary Lucy is not presented as an especially accomplished pianist – 'she struck no more right notes than was suitable for her age and situation' – but she finds an escape from everyday concerns in music and plays Beethoven with triumphant abandon. Mr Beebe remarks that if she 'ever takes to live as she plays it will be very exciting – both for us and for her' (p.32). At the end

---

Build critical skills

Mr Emerson quotes from *A Shropshire Lad* (1896) by A.E. Housman (1859–1936). Hugely popular in Forster's time, Housman was an atheist whose poetry was often a wistful evocation of the anxiety and disappointment of youth. Think about Forster's presentation of Mr Emerson's radical socialist and atheist views here. Note that while characters such as Mr Eager regard themselves as far more cultured than Mr Emerson and sneer at him, this only reflects the poorly chosen criteria upon which their judgements are based. How far do you agree that Mr Emerson's radical modern view of the world is the one Forster himself favours?

of the chapter Mr Beebe, with delightful irony, attributes her independent, arguably rebellious, decision to go out walking in the city alone to 'too much Beethoven' (p.39).

The conversation, once Lucy has stopped playing, focuses on the developing friendship between Charlotte and Miss Lavish who is, it seems, writing a flamboyant novel about life in modern Italy – yet another irony since, in this same chapter, Forster also stresses how little most of these tourists have, or want, to do with the real Italy, real Italians or everyday Italian life. Mr Beebe gently mocks Miss Alan and her blinkered attitude: 'The Italians are a most unpleasant people. They pry everywhere, they see everything and they know what we want before we know it ourselves. We are at their mercy' (p.34). He continues, tongue-in-cheek, to talk of the nation which produced scientific and artistic geniuses such as Galileo and Leonardo da Vinci as having 'no conception of the intellectual life' (p.35).

Forster uses Miss Alan here to represent the middle-class mind-set in which everything is unquestioned and rigid. Miss Alan is, for example, horrified and outraged – or says she is, although her discussing it at length is a sign that she's relishing being judgemental – that Mr Emerson has used the word 'stomach' (p.36) in public and to a lady. And we hear about Miss Lavish, more snobbish, patronising and condescending even than the Miss Alans, ironically commending 'plain speaking' while talking about her brothers who always make a point of 'talking to commercial travellers', as if they are cultural anthropologists studying some arcane savage tribe.

Lucy is still struggling to decide what she should think about the Emersons. Just as she was at a loss to decide in Santa Croce without her trusty Baedeker instructing her what she should admire, so now she asks Mr Beebe: 'old Mr Emerson, is he nice or not nice? I do so want to know' (p.37). Seemingly unable to rely on her own instincts, she also asks Miss Alan before eventually tentatively concluding that 'the Emersons were nice' (p.38). The word 'nice' here is heavily freighted with meaning. It doesn't mean just pleasant, generous or friendly, because Mr Emerson has already proved himself all of those things; it also carries heavy implications of social class, in terms of being suitable, safe or appropriate to associate with.

Build critical skills

Lucy plays the first movement of a Beethoven sonata written just five years before the composer's death in 1827, when he had extreme hearing problems. It is considered one of his more passionate and difficult works. With its 'roar' of an 'opening theme', Lucy surprises Mr Beebe firstly by choosing it and secondly by playing the 'chords that herald the conclusion' as 'hammer-strokes of victory' (p.31). Look closely at how Forster uses the music to externalise Lucy's inner conflict.

Context

Before World War I, respectable women were not expected to smoke at all and gentlemen did not smoke in front of ladies. They were required to retire - typically after dinner - to a smoking room, as the Emersons do at the Pension Bertolini. Miss Lavish is deliberately flouting social convention by entering the male enclave of the smoking room. After World War I, smoking became more acceptable for both sexes.

Chapter 4: Fourth Chapter

Disturbed by her playing of the Beethoven sonata and hungry for adventure, Lucy walks to the centre of the city where she buys postcards of several famous artworks. Then she sees a group of Italians arguing and witnesses a fatal stabbing; George Emerson carries her to safety when she faints. He insists on escorting her back to the pension, having thrown her retrieved but blood-stained postcards into the River Arno.

Context

The street murder in this chapter is a rare moment that suggests that there might be a darker side to the real Italy than is generally seen in the novel. In the early 1900s, this only recently united country was in trouble. Millions of Italians emigrated to the USA, tired of the grinding poverty and lack of opportunity at home. Deep fissures opened up in Italian society: between the richer industrialised North and the poorer agricultural South; the Catholic Church and the state; the landowners and the peasants. Within the novel, Mr Emerson is clearly the only character who might be aware of - or interested in - these socio-political issues.

Commentary Confused and disturbed by the Grundyish norms and values of conventional society, Lucy is increasingly tempted to go her own way. She wants something to happen to her – and follow her own emotions sometimes, rather than just doing as she's told. She wishes something would happen to her – and it does.

This chapter is a turning point in the novel because it is the first time Lucy is alone with George. That is partly why Forster gives the chapter a jokey title – the first three have been titled with apparent trivia; this one really matters and so doesn't have a title at all. She and George witness a dramatic and violent murder that galvanises an irreversible change in them both. The gruesome and pointless death of a stranger makes Lucy see that life is far more complex than she has always been led to believe, and this gradual realisation forces her to question her faith in the norms and values of her enclosed and inward-looking society. Lucy is ready to rebel, setting out to explore the city alone for the first time while 'in her heart … are springing up strange desires' (p.40). Before long those strange desires are partly fulfilled. 'One man was stabbed and another held her in his arms' (p.42). Lucy is attracted to George, fails to understand 'the unexpected melody' in her ears and tries to repel him. First she tells him she can get home without assistance and then she fears that he will say something even more inappropriate: 'Something warned Lucy that she must stop him' (p.45).

Forster leaves us to make up our own minds about the odds of George's appearance at the most opportune moment being mere random chance. Had he followed Lucy protectively, spotting that she was going out alone, or was his presence at the murder scene simply a matter of random chance? The former possibility doesn't occur to Lucy.

Lucy has to face something truly dangerous for the first time in her life in this chapter. It isn't the murder of an unknown stranger itself, of course; that savage event is someone else's tragedy. Far more disturbing to her personal equilibrium is George Emerson. Lucy interprets him as though still looking at a Renaissance Italian painting: '**He lacked chivalry; his thoughts, like his behaviour, would not be modified by awe.** It was useless to say to him, "And would you—" and hope that he would complete the sentence for himself, averting his eyes from her nakedness like the knight in that beautiful picture.' Yet the reader has noticed how George disposes of her art postcards by dropping them into the Arno because they are stained with blood. The symbolism is clear. George will drag Lucy away from looking at pictures that record images of other people's lives and force her to start living for herself.

Top ten quotation

TASK

How does Forster signal the stirrings of something conventionally forbidden between Lucy and George? Look carefully at the end of Chapter 4 and make notes as you try to apply a feminist critical reading to this part of the text.

Chapter 5: Possibilities of a Pleasant Outing

Lucy chooses to spend the morning shopping with Charlotte because, for reasons she doesn't fully understand, she feels uncomfortable about accepting an invitation to walk up to Torre del Gallo with Mr Beebe and the Emersons. They meet Mr Eager who invites them to drive with him to Fiesole, out in the idyllic Tuscan countryside, later in the week.

Commentary Forster uses this chapter to reveal more about the distinctly unpleasant Mr Eager, presented as a clear contrast to the urbane and tactful Mr Beebe. He is, for example, rude and dismissive of the Italian street vendor and cavalierly snobbish about Mr Emerson's profession as a journalist (p.54). He also tries to spread malicious gossip by suggesting that Mr Emerson murdered his late wife – notice the way in which the three statements he makes are progressively toned down. While Charlotte's faulty judgement causes her to revere him because he represents the English community in Florence, Lucy, at last, and despite her fear that 'it was too dreadful not to know whether she was thinking right or wrong', is beginning to wake up. She quietly doubts that Miss Lavish, whom the three of them have been discussing, is in fact 'a great artist' or that 'Mr Eager is as full of spirituality and culture as she had been led to suppose'. Soon Forster tells us that 'Lucy's rebellious thoughts swept out in words – for the first time in her life' as she stands up to Mr Eager, indignantly challenging his poisonous hints about Mr Emerson. Yet she still has some way to go. Before long we see here 'losing her courage, and relapsing into the old chaotic methods' (p.54).

The trip which Mr Eager is planning – and which takes place in the next chapter – is pivotal to the plot of the novel, so Chapter 5 functions as an important narrative signpost. It is also in this chapter that the reader first hears of the Vyse family. A letter from Lucy's mother informs her that the Vyses have gone to Rome, even if this is 'the news that interests her least' (p.58). Their presence in Rome does, however, make Lucy think about leaving Florence and moving on to join these neighbours from Surrey. Thus, from the very first mention of him, Cecil represents that side of Lucy's personality that is backward-looking and determined to play things safe rather than remain where she is and grapple with her growing feelings for George.

That Lucy herself doesn't understand or recognise what is happening to her at this point in the novel – although the reader most certainly does – is another sign of the extent to which her natural feelings have to be artificially suppressed. The Austrian neurologist Sigmund Freud (1856–1939) attached great significance to the underlying hidden meanings of words and actions and interpreted them as clues that could uncover the essential truth about a patient's state of mind. The famous 'Freudian slip', for example, is a mistake (often a speech error or 'slip of the tongue') that actually shows up a conflict between expected 'correct' patterns of behaviour and the hidden desires of the individual. Freud's theories were already well-known among intellectual and academic circles by 1908, and Forster certainly makes use of his ideas in his presentation of Lucy's psychology here and elsewhere in the novel.

Taking it further ▷

English people have chosen to settle permanently or semi-permanently in Florence since the early eighteenth century – to work, for its art, architecture, culture, climate, way or life and more. Forster refers to it as 'the English colony in Florence'. There is, for example, an English cemetery in the city where famous ex-patriates such as the nineteenth-century poet Elizabeth Barrett Browning are buried. You might enjoy watching Franco Zeffirelli's film *Tea with Mussolini* (1999), which depicts life among a group of English ex-pats in Florence in the period before World War I.

Chapter 6: The Reverend Arthur Beebe, The Reverend Cuthbert Eager, Mr Emerson, Mr George Emerson, Miss Eleanor Lavish, Miss Charlotte Bartlett and Miss Lucy Honeychurch Drive Out in Carriages to See a View

The planned afternoon visit to Fiesole takes place in two carriages because the party has expanded to include Miss Lavish and the Emersons – a development which fazes both Lucy and Mr Eager for different reasons. There is a disagreement about the appropriateness of the coach driver's

Taking it further ▷

You might enjoy comparing Forster's method of characterising the narrow-minded and spiteful Mr Eager in this chapter with Jane Austen's characterisation of her equally snobbish and unpleasant clerics Mr Collins in *Pride and Prejudice* and Mr Elton in *Emma*. Forster often lets Mr Eager condemn himself out of his own mouth. His dialogue is all that is needed; authorial comment is unnecessary.

Context

Florence is a city surrounded by hills. Fiesole is a hilltop village, eight kilometres to the north-east which affords good views of the city. Today it is a pretty commercialised tourist spot and has grown into a small town - although it can still be approached only via a winding road uphill. In Forster's time it was quite rural and unspoiled.

being accompanied by an attractive young woman. Once the party reaches its destination and temporarily disperses, Lucy finds herself very briefly alone in a field of violets with George – who kisses her.

Context

Alessio Baldovinetti (1425-99), whom Mr Eager and Miss Lavish chatter about on the way to Fiesole, was an early Renaissance Florentine painter credited with developing the concept of landscape painting.

Build critical skills

Mr Eager's remark about being treated 'as if we were a party of Cook's tourists' is another marker of his unpleasant snobbery. Thomas Cook (1808–92) invented mass tourism by taking people on package trips first in Britain and then abroad. He made travel possible for the masses when previously only the wealthy could afford to travel for pleasure. Contrast Mr Eager's attitude with the way Lucy deliberately describes herself as a 'tourist'. Consider why Forster has her do this.

Commentary This chapter is pivotal in *A Room with a View*. George makes his feelings openly clear; seeing Lucy appear 'enveloped' in 'light and beauty' on a 'little open terrace … covered with violets from end to end' he knows exactly what to do. 'Courage!' he calls, 'Courage and love', showing he is truly his father's son. Forster's description of this first kiss will repay several close readings. The picture of this beautiful young woman stumbling out of a shady wood into the bright Italian sunlight is one of romantic perfection – yet Lucy has no time to work out what she feels about George's passionate kiss before they are discovered. Charlotte arrives amid the glorious violets, wrecking the perfection of the moment as she stands out 'brown against the view'.

Lucy has been struggling with her developing feelings for George to the point where 'each time she avoided George it became more imperative that she should avoid him again' (p.61). She is aware that there had been intimate, unspoken communication between them beside the Arno after the street murder in Chapter 4. George, for his part, has already shown 'in an open manner' that he wants 'to continue their intimacy'. Lucy is uneasy because 'she did not know what had happened, and suspected that he did know. And this frightened her' (p.61).

Elsewhere in this chapter we see the little drama of the Italian coach driver and his girl. Unlike George, he can show what he feels for his girlfriend by putting his arm round her and would happily kiss her in public were it not for the (subliminally jealous?) interference of Mr Eager. Note that the always rational and humane Mr Emerson takes issue with Mr Eager for interfering; he has 'parted two people who were happy' (p.65). This division of the young Italian lovers, nicknamed Phaethon and Persephone, is an example of proleptic irony or foreshadowing; soon it will be Mr Emerson's own son and Lucy who are 'parted'.

The coachman's pretended misunderstanding of *buoni uomini* – good men – is a fairly heavy-handed piece of dramatic irony. The reader can see the misunderstanding but Lucy cannot. She means the two clergymen, Mr Eager and Mr Beebe, but the perceptive and sensitive coach driver has observed that the two *really* 'good men' in the party are the Emersons, so directs her to them. He has also spotted the burgeoning attraction between George and Lucy so to him it is just common sense to bring them together. 'Phaethon', who is despised as a vulgar peasant by the likes of Mr Eager, shows a perceptive sensitivity towards his English counterparts, whose class and culture make them far less able to express their emotions openly and honestly.

Chapter 7: They Return

The party reconvenes and begins the return to the city without George Emerson, who chooses to walk. A severe thunderstorm with heavy rain makes the return journey uncomfortable. Worried that both the cab driver and George will talk about the kiss, Charlotte gives the driver a coin to buy his silence. After a long discussion with Lucy in the privacy of Charlotte's bedroom it is agreed – with confused reluctance on Lucy's part – that Charlotte will confront George Emerson when he eventually gets back to the Pension Bertolini. Lucy hears Charlotte intercept George and ask to speak to him downstairs.

Commentary Thunderstorms are traditionally associated with breaking passion in literature and here Forster makes satiric use of the literary technique of the pathetic fallacy. The storm symbolises Lucy's tumultuous emotional experience with George and her feelings about it – as well as affording Forster the opportunity to put more glib platitudes into the mouth of the sanctimonious Mr Eager. The whole group, for different reasons, has a 'general sense of groping and bewilderment' at the end of this afternoon of 'social contretemps and unsuccessful picnics' (p.71). The most heart-warming feeling expressed is Mr Emerson's serious worry – with which nobody else sympathises much – about George's safety out alone on a lonely hillside in a thunderstorm.

During the long wet evening which follows, Lucy tells Charlotte that she intends to speak to George about what has happened. While Charlotte is convinced that George with his 'deplorable antecedents and education' will gossip about kissing Lucy as one of his 'exploits', Lucy knows instinctively that he will not: 'I have a feeling that talk is a thing he will never do' (p.76). When asked what would have happened if Charlotte had not appeared at the moment of the hillside kiss, Lucy says, several times that she 'can't think'. On one level this simply means that Lucy genuinely doesn't know, on another it indicates that she is so muddled by her feelings for George that she can't think straight about anything. Obeying Charlotte's instructions about coming away from the window – and thus, of course, turning away from the open *view* to face inwards into the enclosed *room* – Lucy starts packing for the move to Rome. This cop-out solution will protect her from having to work out her own views on the momentous event that has just occurred.

Forster does not tell us exactly what Charlotte says to George. Like Lucy, we hear him arrive – presumably weary, wet and thoughtful – and we hear Charlotte ask him to come downstairs. Then Lucy hears him trudge past her door

Build critical skills

Forster calls the coach driver Phaethon, son of the god Apollo in Greek mythology. His lover is nicknamed Persephone, daughter of Zeus, king of the gods. The story is that on one occasion Phaethon was allowed to drive Apollo's sun chariot – with awful results. Persephone was abducted while gathering flowers and taken to the underworld, but because of an eventual compromise to allow her back annually for a few months, she personifies vegetation and spring. Consider why Forster chooses such significant nick names for the young lovers.

Context

▲ Laurence Fox as Cecil in the 2007 ITV film

with 'heavy and tired breathing'. She is clearly still yearning for something she doesn't understand – a subtle depiction of gradual sexual awakening. 'It isn't true, it can't all be true. I want not to be muddled', she cries aloud. This chapter marks the end of Part One and Lucy's time in Florence. Forster has – for the moment – separated her from George.

TASK

Study closely the passage in this chapter about the thunderstorm from 'Rain and darkness came on together' to '…vast possibilities of good' (pp.72–3). Write detailed notes on the methods Forster uses to present this key scene.

Part Two

Chapter 8: Medieval

About four months have passed since Lucy and Charlotte left Florence, since when they have been touring Rome and the Alps with Cecil Vyse and his mother. Cecil is now in the garden at Windy Corner, the Honeychurches' home in Surrey, proposing marriage to Lucy for the third time. Neither Mrs Honeychurch nor Lucy's brother Freddy, who are in the drawing room awaiting the outcome of the proposal, are especially pleased about the prospect of this marriage, although they pretend to themselves and each other that they don't much mind either way. Mr Beebe arrives and is disappointed to hear that Lucy has agreed to marry Cecil, although by the end of the chapter there is a celebratory atmosphere at Windy Corner.

Commentary Cecil Vyse, who is presented 'thus late in the story', is the antithesis of George and the reader is led to wonder why Lucy has already turned him down twice. Significantly, Forster informs the reader of this significant fact almost in passing, by means of a throwaway comment from Freddy: 'It's his third go, isn't it?' In this way many questions are raised as to how, in the four months since she left Florence, Lucy has somehow managed to dampen down the torrent of emotions that was then unleashed and force herself to play by the safe rules of her culture and class. Mrs Honeychurch describes Cecil as good, clever, rich and well connected, while the narrator informs the reader that he is 'well educated, well endowed and not deficient physically'. It seems everyone is looking for positive things to say about Cecil to offset their underlying reservations.

In fact, Cecil's condescending snobbery comes across very clearly in this chapter. He sneers at the Honeychurches taking care of their new carpet and sees their recently bought furniture as vulgar; upper-class families like his own have heirloom antiques. He privately vows to introduce Lucy 'into more congenial circles as soon as possible'. Cecil has no profession, as he tells Mr Beebe, and criticises Freddy who is training to be a doctor (hence his anatomy book and bone). He also makes Mr Beebe feel awkward and uncomfortable by allowing him to talk at length about Lucy's passionate piano-playing and its effect on her life before mentioning that she is now his fiancée.

This chapter makes it clear to the reader that Cecil is an unsuitable match for Lucy. While they have known each other for several years, it was only when they got to know each other better in Rome that Cecil saw she might make him a suitable wife. The contrast between Cecil's tepid affection and George Emerson's passionate love is stark. Yet no one is forcing Lucy to marry him; indeed Mrs Honeychurch considers telling Mrs Vyse that Lucy 'seems very uncertain, and in these days young people must decide for themselves' (p. 89).

Chapter 9: Lucy as a Work of Art

Lucy and her mother take Cecil to a garden party which he detests. On the way back via the village they talk to their neighbour, Sir Harry Otway, about the two newly built 'vulgar' houses he has bought near the church. One still needs a tenant and Lucy suggests the Miss Alans. Walking home from the village through the woods alone with Lucy, Cecil kisses her for the first time. It is not a success.

Commentary The word 'fiasco', as Forster explains, is a Honeychurch family in-joke term meaning 'fiancé'. Thus when Forster refers to 'Lucy and her Fiasco' in the opening sentence of this chapter, the irony is obvious: Lucy's engagement to Cecil is so inappropriate – by any standard other than the shallow conventional one – that it is a *real* fiasco.

Context

The word 'fiasco' began as Victorian theatre slang for a disastrous stage flop. It is derived from the Italian *far fiasco*, meaning to utterly break down in performance. This term is highly relevant, given the fact that Cecil is only acting the part of Lucy's passionate fiancé as opposed to really feeling it.

Context

In the second half of the nineteenth and early twentieth centuries, London's Tottenham Court Road (p.92) became associated with stylish modern furniture shops. The most famous was Heal's, which is still there, although it now occupies a smaller space than originally. Cecil's snobbery is because people like the Honeychurches don't have precious inherited antique furniture, so have to buy theirs new.

Attending the garden party as Lucy's fiancé and being fussed over by 'smirking old women' is a very ordinary social occasion, yet Cecil describes the experience, with laughable hyperbole, as 'appalling, disastrous, portentous' and finds it 'disgusting' that his engagement is now regarded as 'public property'. Lucy who had 'rather enjoyed herself' at the party struggles to understand why he is so irritated. Cecil's response is to talk down to her in a pseudo-intellectual manner he knows she will not fully understand. This leads her to mention her passionate dislike of Mr Eager, and also the Emersons, whom Mr Eager took such pleasure in castigating in Florence. Significantly she gives Mr Emerson a false name, perhaps because at some subconscious level she doesn't want to reveal too much about her feelings for him – and by extension George – to Cecil.

Top ten quotation

But it is such an awkward size. It is too large for the peasant class and too small for anyone in the least like ourselves.

Cecil, however, is nothing like as clever and knowledgeable as he wants Lucy and everyone else to think he is. He bungles an art history reference by claiming that Leonardo da Vinci painted the Sistine Chapel ceiling in Rome when in fact it was Michelangelo, and Mrs Honeychurch manages not to comment when he speaks of the deciduous larch tree as an evergreen. 'Occasionally he went wrong in a question of fact', as the narrator observes. We see his judgemental snobbery as he derides the pair of new semi-detached villas which have 'spoiled' the village. He suggests 'maliciously' that the untenanted house would be 'a perfect paradise for a bank clerk' in response to Sir Harry Otway's assertion that 'it would too small for anyone the least like ourselves' (p.107).

The most telling moment in this chapter is, however, Cecil's attempt to kiss Lucy, apparently generated in part by a revealing conversation they have just had while walking in the woods near her home:

'Which way shall we go?' she asked him.

Nature – simplest of topics, she thought – was around them. Summer Street lay deep in the woods, and she had stopped where a footpath diverged from the highroad.

'Are there two ways?'

'Perhaps the road is more sensible, as we're got up smart.'

'I'd rather go through the wood,' said Cecil, with that subdued irritation that she had noticed in him all the afternoon. 'Why is it, Lucy, that you always say the road? Do you know that you have never once been with me in the fields or the wood since we were engaged?'

'Haven't I? The wood, then,' said Lucy, startled at his queerness, but pretty sure that he would explain later; it was not his habit to leave her in doubt as to his meaning.

She led the way into the whispering pines, and sure enough he did explain before they had gone a dozen yards.

'I had got an idea – I dare say wrongly – that you feel more at home with me in a room.'

'A room?' she echoed, hopelessly bewildered.

'Yes. Or, at the most, in a garden, or on a road. Never in the real country like this.'

'Oh, Cecil, whatever do you mean? I have never felt anything of the sort. You talk as if I was a kind of poetess sort of person.'

'I don't know that you aren't. I connect you with a view – a certain type of view. Why shouldn't you connect me with a room?'

She reflected a moment, and then said, laughing:

'Do you know that you're right? I do. I must be a poetess after all. When I think of you it's always as in a room. How funny!'

To her surprise, he seemed annoyed.

'A drawing-room, pray? With no view?'

'Yes, with no view, I fancy. Why not?'

'I'd rather,' he said reproachfully, 'that you connected me with the open air.'

She said again, 'Oh, Cecil, whatever do you mean?'

(p.110)

It is important to compare Cecil's kiss with George's spontaneous gesture at Fiesole. Notice how awkwardly Cecil asks Lucy's permission, how clumsily self-conscious he is, and how comically his pince-nez glasses get knocked off. 'Passion', Forster comments, tacitly inviting the reader to make comparisons between Lucy's two lovers, 'should never ask for leave where there is a right of way' (p.113). Cecil is aware that this significant moment has failed and is puzzled, since 'any labourer or navvy' would have done better. The reader gets the impression that he doesn't really want to kiss Lucy at all and is only going through the motions because it's expected of him; he even finds time 'to wish that he could recoil'. For her part Lucy, blushing and embarrassed, submits because this is what engagement and marriage means but the 'businesslike lift to her veil' indicates her emotional detachment (p.112).

As they walk on homeward Lucy tells Cecil Mr Emerson's real name – perhaps because she feels she should deal with him honestly and speak the truth. After the failed kiss, however, there is a great deal left unspoken between them.

Chapter 10: Cecil as a Humorist

Cecil, has, by chance, encountered the Emersons in the National Gallery and arranged with Sir Harry Otway for them to take the tenancy of the vacant villa instead of the Miss Alans. His aim is to stir up trouble among the snobbish villagers to amuse himself at their expense. Lucy discovers this through a chance remark of Freddy's and is very annoyed with Cecil.

Commentary At this half-way point in the novel Forster reveals Lucy's precise social background. Her late father was a successful solicitor – a man who, like the Emersons, had to work for a living. The presence of his middle-class family in a now desirable part of the Surrey Weald, where many newer neighbouring houses have since been bought by people with inherited wealth, stems from a lucky early investment in a house there by Mr Honeychurch before the area became sought after. Lucy is often wrongly assumed, by the neighbours, to be 'the remnants of an indigenous aristocracy'. Having grown up rooted 'in the best society obtainable' and all its prejudices, Italy has given her 'new eyes'. She now believes that 'there was no one whom she might not get to like' (pp.114–15). Forster describes Lucy as a 'rebel' here, 'but not of the kind he [Cecil] understood – a rebel who desired, not a wider dwelling room, but equality beside the man she loved. For Italy was offering her the most priceless of possessions – her own soul' (p.115).

Top ten quotation

> A Radical out and out, she learned to speak with horror of Suburbia. Life as far as she troubled to conceive it, was a circle of rich, pleasant people with identical interests and identical foes. In this circle one thought, married and died. Outside it were poverty and vulgarity.

Yet Cecil has also acquired a different outlook since his return from Italy. Despising, and irritated by, the narrowness of the local social set, he seeks to replace it in his life and Lucy's to stir things up. He finds people like the Emersons amusing and treats them as playthings by arranging for them to come to Summer Street as a way of playing a smug trick on the locals and hopefully stirring up some social awkwardness. Forster is gradually revealing the depth of the incompatibility between Lucy and Cecil, who takes 'a malicious delight in thwarting people' (p.119).

We also see Lucy and Cecil completely misunderstanding each other. At first she thinks the new tenants are friends of Cecil's and realises she has nothing to worry about, apart from the disappointment of the Miss Alans (p.118). When she realises that she won't be able to avoid seeing George again, however, she is furious. The class-obsessed Cecil, not knowing anything about the events in Florence, mistakes this for 'snobbery' on Lucy's part and declares with unconscious irony that 'There ought to be intermarriage – all that sort of thing. I believe in democracy' (p.122).

Forster is at his comic best in this chapter as Freddy struggles to remember the names of the new tenants. Forster's use of dramatic irony ensures that the reader sees what's coming before Lucy does.

Chapter 11: In Mrs Vyse's Well-Appointed Flat

Lucy and Cecil are staying with his mother in her London flat. Meanwhile the Emersons have moved to Summer Street. A letter from Charlotte, pretentiously addressed to 'Dearest Lucia', advises Lucy to tell her mother and Cecil about George Emerson's actions in Florence which irritates Lucy greatly. She writes back at once saying it is far too late to tell her mother now, and forcefully telling her to drop the subject. Mrs Vyse is kind to Lucy when the latter wakes with a nightmare.

Commentary This short chapter, unusually, presents Lucy in a different environment. She is in London, not Italy or Surrey. We hear Cecil in private conversation with his mother after Lucy has gone to bed, agreeing that 'the Honeychurch taint' – by which they mean her middle-class social roots – is disappearing and that she is 'becoming wonderful'. Mrs Vyse wants Cecil to make Lucy 'one of us' as soon as possible and notes with approval that she is no longer 'always quoting servants, and asking one how pudding is made'.

Context

Showing off to Lucy, the smirking Cecil mentions having had a victory for 'the Comic Muse' in persuading Sir Harry Otway to rent his cottage to the Emersons. In Greek mythology each of the nine muses inspires a different art form; for example, art, music or literature. The muses, all daughters of Zeus and Memory, are supernatural personifications from whom ideas flow. The muse for comedy is Thalia and Cecil mentions the novelist George Meredith (1928-09) who suggested that humour and truth are the same.

Lucy plays Schumann at a dinner party Mrs Vyse has organised and refuses to play Beethoven – which is becoming a symbol of passion and abandon. Lucy is controlling her innermost feelings here and Forster jokes that Mr Beebe would never have said 'too much Schumann' because this music is more restrained and disciplined.

The dinner party itself is a satire. So concerned is Mrs Vyse to keep up social class appearances that everyone she has invited or managed to 'scrape together' seems to be the grandchild of someone famous. The result is 'witty weariness' in conversation, which is novel to Lucy (p.126).

Charlotte's intrusive, grating letter reveals that she and Lucy ceased to get on well together after leaving Florence. Now, with her usual whingeing **prurience**, she advises Lucy to tell her mother and Cecil about George's insult. She clearly thinks the Emersons have deliberately come to Summer Street to cause trouble and wants to avoid any possible blame attaching to her if the story of the kiss gets out. Lucy writes back quite crossly. Significantly Forster describes Lucy 'and her secret' staying in London for another ten days after the arrival of the letter, as if her memory of George's kiss is a physical presence or living entity. The impossibility of forgetting what has happened emerges in Lucy's nightmare at the end of the chapter, through which (of course) Cecil snores on obliviously. Lucy is still deeply troubled at the situation in which she finds herself.

prurience: officious and interfering behaviour.

Chapter 12: Twelfth Chapter

Mr Beebe and Freddy visit the Emersons who are moving into their villa. Freddy invites George to go swimming with him in a pond in the woods and they persuade Mr Beebe to join them. Boyish horseplay ensues and leads to the scattering of all three piles of clothes and scampering round the pond undressed. Mrs Honeychurch, Lucy and Cecil arrive at the pool on their way to visit a neighbour.

Commentary This is the first time Lucy and George have seen each other since Florence and it is significant that he is 'Barefoot, bare-chested, radiant and personable' unlike fussy Cecil who 'always felt that he must lead women, though he knew not whither, and protect them, though he knew not what against' (p.137). Forster doesn't tell us what Lucy is really feeling although the description of her through Cecil's eyes is significant; she 'was all parasol and evidently "minded"' (Chapter 12). Cecil interprets this deliberate hiding of her face behind her parasol as connoting her virginal embarrassment and confusion, but since Lucy used to swim naked in this very pond with Freddy as children, she is unlikely to be embarrassed in the way Cecil thinks she is – that is, by the sight of a naked man. Indeed after an art history tour around Italy, Lucy has surely seen many naked men – albeit in statue form. What shocks her into silence and an urgent need to cover her face is the sight of the handsome George undressed.

The Emersons have no servants which marks them out as different from the Honeychurches and Vyses. When Freddy and Mr Beebe arrive George is moving

Context

Götterdämmerung (1874) is a huge scale opera by Richard Wagner, the fourth and last work in The Ring Cycle. The cycle opens and closes grandly with maidens in the River Rhine with which Forster, ridiculously, is comparing Freddy, George and Mr Beebe bathing in their tiny, reed-clogged pond.

furniture himself although he hasn't yet got round to taking the wardrobe upstairs (p.129). It also makes him seem more masculine than most of the other men in the book. Left in the sitting room on their own both Mr Beebe and Freddy are struck by the number and variety of the Emersons' books. Mr Beebe is inclined to sneer. Freddy wishes rather wistfully that he could, as Lucy is learning to with Cecil, read 'books that you can talk about afterwards' (p.130).

Mr Emerson's perceptive, outspoken 'philosophy' – such as his comment about the Garden of Eden on page 131 – makes others feel uncomfortable. Freddy, for instance, is 'appalled at the mass of philosophy that was approaching him'.

The idea of three adult men, one of them an older clergyman, cavorting naked only to be stumbled upon by two ladies and their escort who suffers from 'prudishness' is a set-piece of situation comedy. From the moment Mr Beebe strips and walks away from his clothes the reader knows that something of the sort is coming. The frolicking is innocently boyish, the pond is 'a momentary chalice for youth' (p.136). Forster tells us that 'they forgot Italy and Botany and Fate' and simply 'began to play'. Even Mrs Honeychurch isn't really offended, just concerned that they should dry themselves properly to avoid catching cold; she finds it 'impossible to remain shocked'. Lucy meanwhile wants to get away because she has seen George. The fact that she can think of no suitable reaction other than bowing shows how inadequate her social training is to equip her to deal with the sight of the handsome young man she is trying not to love appearing naked before her (p.138).

Chapter 13: How Miss Bartlett's Boiler Was So Tiresome

After observing Cecil's rudeness to a lady the three of them visited in the village after the pond incident, Mrs Honeychurch tells Lucy that she is increasingly concerned about Cecil's manners. When Lucy tries to distract her by mentioning the letter from Charlotte, Mrs Honeychurch insists that Charlotte be invited to stay while the plumbers fix her leaky boiler. Freddy meanwhile wants to invite the Emersons for tennis.

CRITICAL VIEW

The poet and critic T.S. Eliot coined the term 'objective correlative' to describe the way in which objects, situations or events can be used in literature to represent characters or emotions. It seems Forster is using Charlotte's leaky boiler - 'so tiresome' - as a comic objective correlative for her own annoying personality, which always threatens to do something exasperating at a time that causes maximum inconvenience to everyone else.

Commentary Forster begins to make quite clear in this chapter the attraction to George which Lucy is trying to suppress. She has evidently thought about him and tried to imagine circumstances in which they might meet again. What discomposes her is that when she did meet George he was 'happy' enough to greet her with 'the shout of a morning star'. Lucy continues to think about this all the time she is at Mrs Butterworth's house with Cecil and her mother although 'her faculties were busy with Cecil' (p.139).

It is also evident here that the relationship with Cecil is so flawed that even Mrs Honeychurch, having previously shown 'charity and restraint', begins to hint at reservations 'with gathering displeasure' (p.140). When Lucy tries feebly to defend Cecil her mother replies tartly: 'If high ideals make a man rude then the sooner he gets rid of them the better' (p.140) She is aware that things at Windy Corner make Cecil 'wince' (p.141) and that he disapproves of her family's way of life and even their furniture, 'wriggling and sneering and spoiling everyone's pleasure' when Freddy sings. Lucy is embarrassed partly because she cannot find a good argument in favour of Cecil's superciliousness. After a bit Mrs Honeychurch stops expressing criticism, embraces Lucy and makes peace with her (p.143) but at the same time presses the point that Charlotte, who has problems with the plumbing in her own home, must be invited to stay.

Lucy argues strongly against this partly because she and Cecil both dislike Charlotte and find her very trying but also – although she is unable to admit this to herself – because Charlotte knows about the incident with George in Florence. She is, moreover, unable to dissuade Freddy from inviting the Emersons to Windy Corner because she can't give him a reason. 'All this muddle' and 'it's better not' (p.142) do nothing to convince him.

At the end of the chapter Cecil, annoyed by what he regards as the Honeychurches' vulgar and trivial concerns ('eggs, boilers, hydrangeas, maids'), addresses Mrs Honeychurch with the 'scarcely veiled insolence' that she has been complaining to Lucy about earlier (p.147). The subtle gradations of the class system are at work again.

> ## Build critical skills
>
> Lucy's evasions and excuses here only serve to heighten the reader's awareness of the extent to which she is repressing a complex cocktail of thoughts and feelings. Taking a psychoanalytical approach here may reveal how Forster creates distance between Lucy and the reader that sheds light on her intensifying emotional crisis.

> ## TASK
>
> Summarise, with brief supporting quotations, Mrs Honeychurch's reservations and concerns about Cecil's behaviour.

> ## TASK
>
> As a widow, Marian Honeychurch has full control over Windy Corner and makes decisions which would be her husband's if he were still alive. She never defers to Freddy as the 'man of the house' and they are both amused in Chapter 8 that Cecil asks Freddy's permission (as well as Mrs Honeychurch's) to marry Lucy. Forster thus presents Mrs Honeychurch as a competent manager of her own house who is, however, scathing about female equality and wants her daughter to make a conventional marriage (although not to Cecil Vyse). What might a feminist interpretation of her paradoxical views be?

Chapter 14: How Lucy Faced the External Situation Bravely

The chapter begins with an analysis of Lucy's complex emotional state before Charlotte arrives and bores everyone at Windy Corner with her tiresome attempts to pay her own cab fare. Lucy assures Charlotte that she has met and spoken with George and that she is certain he will tell no one about their kiss in Florence.

Commentary Lucy continues to be attracted to George whose 'voice moved her deeply and she wished to remain near him' (p.148). Forster's authorial voice acknowledges that, while it may be obvious to the reader what is happening, it is still not obvious to Lucy. As the week wears on the reader is informed that **'more of her defences fell and she entertained an image that had physical beauty'** (p.149) as Forster develops the reader's awareness of Lucy's sexual awakening.

> **Top ten quotation**

The infuriating Charlotte is true to form in this chapter. Catching the wrong train means that she has 'contrived to bungle her arrival' (p.149) and missed Mrs Honeychurch who has gone to the station to meet her. Nearly four exquisitely excruciating pages are given to her attempts to pay for the cab she has had to take and the young people gathered in the garden enjoy making it worse for her. Freddy and Cecil are for once on the same side as they lark about and make her look silly. The humorous situational irony here stems from Charlotte's being the only character present who can't see what's going on.

Once alone with Lucy, Charlotte immediately asks about George. Lucy tries to convince her cousin (and herself) that everything is all right. However, she knows that, even if Cecil knew, he wouldn't laugh it off 'for he desired her untouched' (p.152). Thus Forster continues to develop Cecil's character as a man completely unsuitable for Lucy.

Lucy reassures Charlotte, who states 'once a cad, always a cad' twice, that the Emerson situation 'is really all right' (p.153). She then spoils the impression she's trying to create, as Forster gleefully observes, with an image about people looking especially attractive 'against a background of violets' (p.154). The reader is left to speculate as to whether Charlotte has noticed these disconnections and **non sequiturs** when we discover at the very end of the novel that she helped to unite George and Lucy (p.219).

non sequiturs: things that don't follow on logically but that seem random and unconnected.

Chapter 15: The Disaster Within

Lucy attends church with her mother, cousin and Minnie Beebe after which they speak to the Emersons who are in the garden of their house. George agrees to come to Windy Corner for tennis in the afternoon. Cecil, who refuses to play tennis, reads aloud from Miss Lavish's novel, mocking it as he does so. One passage is about a girl being unexpectedly kissed in a field of violets near Florence and Lucy realises with horror that this Miss Lavish has made use of her own experience with George. Lucy is keenly aware of George's physical presence all afternoon at the end of which he corners her and kisses her once again.

Commentary The attendance at church by the women is partly a plot device so that Mrs Honeychurch meets the Emersons conventionally and reinforces the tennis invitation. Forster thus finds a plausible way of getting George to Windy Corner. It also further highlights the cultural gulf between Lucy and Cecil. She attends church as a way of life, 'a natural birthright', rather than out of any deep-felt religious conviction. Cecil doesn't go because he despises this attitude and sneers when they leave although he claims to respect 'honest orthodoxy'. Moreover church is a shallow excuse to dress up. There's a lot of fuss about clothes here, with Charlotte producing a 'lovely frock' and asking with her usual mock-humble self-pity, 'If I did not wear my best rags and tatters now, when should I wear them?' (p.157).

Lucy is trying to allow Cecil to educate her. 'She no longer read novels herself, devoting all her spare time to solid literature in the hope of catching Cecil up', we are told, which implies that Cecil has rather highbrow literary tastes. Yet the only book he is ever seen reading is Miss Lavish's trashy novel, which he mocks superciliously: 'Three split infinitives. Dreadful' (p.163). The reader of course wonders why, if he despises it so much, he doesn't stop reading it and devote himself to something more worthwhile.

The discussion of reading and literature in this chapter is interesting. In the nineteenth century, the only literature studied at university would be in Greek or Latin, as works by English writers were not deemed worthy of academic study. Serious people read poetry but novels were still often regarded as trivial, especially when written by women. Remember that Mary Ann Evans (1819–80) wrote as George Eliot, the Brontë sisters originally published under male pseudonyms and even Miss Lavish's books come out under the name of 'Joseph Emery Prank'. Here we discover that Lucy is now not reading novels any longer, while Cecil declares 'All modern books are bad … Everyone writes for money in these days.' Forster ridicules this ignorant attitude; a new century has dawned and views are changing fast. His own novels were taken very seriously, as were those of contemporaries such as D.H. Lawrence, Virginia Woolf and James Joyce. Moreover, by 1927, Forster was lecturing on English Literature at King's College, Cambridge; the curriculum had altered at last.

This long chapter presents George and Lucy together in an informal setting with other people for the first time since the Fiesole trip in Italy. Lucy is increasingly,

◀ King's College, Cambridge, where Forster was a student and lived as a Fellow in the last third of his life

magnetically, yet still unwillingly, drawn to him. She is influenced by the romantic setting of the English countryside – 'how beautiful the Weald looked' – and compares it with Florence. George talks about views and argues that they don't matter and suddenly we're back at the opening of the novel when George and Lucy first see each other. When George sits on the ground near her chair his head is near her knee. 'She did not want to stroke it, but saw herself wanting to stroke it; the sensation was curious' while George, she notices, is 'a little flushed'. Cecil, meanwhile, continues to make laboured and pretentious comments about the book in his hand and to put the impervious George – 'the man was ill-bred – he hadn't put on his coat after tennis' – firmly in his place as often as possible.

On the way back to the house George spontaneously kisses Lucy when no one else is present. Forster uses the passive voice here, as in 'she … was kissed by him', so the reader is not told at that second exactly how Lucy responded.

Chapter 16: Lying to George

Back in her bedroom, Lucy reflects on the kiss, thinks briefly about what she really feels and suppresses her emotions. She then confronts George in the presence of Charlotte who doesn't want to do the talking. George declares his love and tells Lucy that she shouldn't marry Cecil which Lucy tries to regard as nonsense. Later, when Cecil pompously refuses to play tennis with Freddy, Lucy suddenly recognises him for what he is and breaks off the engagement.

Commentary This chapter continues effectively without a break from where the previous one stopped; the opening sentence begins with a conjunction, 'but', to make the link clear. This is almost the novelistic equivalent of **enjambment** in poetry. It keeps the pace fast and works on the curiosity of the reader.

enjambment: a poetic device whereby the sense of a line or sentence doesn't end at the end of a line of poetry, but runs on over into another one.

Lucy has 'developed since the spring' (p.169). She is deeply drawn to George both with her body and her heart but, 'remembering her engagement to Cecil' believes that she must suppress her feelings; the word 'stifle' occurs twice in the opening paragraph. Forster makes her thought processes clear. She is deluding herself – and lying to George – as the chapter heading has it. Lucy's aim is 'to defeat herself' and she pretends that she has succeeded by assuring herself that 'he was nothing to her; he had never been anything: he had behaved abominably'. Then she tells Charlotte bluntly that 'something too awful has happened' whereas in fact Forster wants us to see past her nervous protestations and to understand something wonderful has happened. Indeed the last lines of the chapter reveal rather brutally how quickly Lucy realises the impossibility of marrying Cecil: 'The scales fell from Lucy's eyes. How had she stood Cecil for a moment? He was absolutely intolerable, and the same evening she broke her engagement off.' As with the end of the previous chapter, Forster makes the reader wait for the details of that interview until the next chapter (Chapter 17 – 'Lying to Cecil') – another example of his deft narrative structure.

Forster continues to develop his characterisation of Charlotte in this chapter. She has done wrong in telling the unreliable, disreputable Eleanor Lavish about

George's kiss, and Lucy is crisply, incisively and justifiably angry. 'Why did you tell her though? This is a most serious thing', she demands before stamping her foot with irritation (p.171). Charlotte winces, as well she might, and squirms with embarrassment when Lucy tries to send George away by being firm and refusing to hear any argument (p.173). George astonishes Lucy with his warm and articulate explanation of why Cecil is not right for her before telling her that he loves her – twice (pp.174 and 175). 'It is our last chance and I shall do all I can', he says, with the same sort of directness the conventional despise in his father.

George states here what Forster has shown the reader all along. Not only is Cecil a small-minded snob who sneers at the innocent mistakes of others (such as Mr Emerson's mispronunciations at the National Gallery); George also sees he wants to indoctrinate Lucy into his own prejudices. Cecil has no concept of allowing a woman to be a decision-making equal and is 'the type who's kept Europe back for a thousand years'. George, however, tells Lucy: 'I want you to have your own thoughts even when I hold you in my arms.'

After George's dignified exit, Charlotte and Lucy apparently rejoice. In terms of the narrative, Charlotte's presence is important here. It means she has heard George's impassioned declaration, which eventually influences her benevolent action at the end of the novel when George realises that she has helped to unite them.

Chapter 17: Lying to Cecil

Lucy explains to Cecil why she is breaking off the engagement late at night when everyone else has gone to bed. She tells him that she isn't well enough educated for him and that she wants to be allowed to think independently. He is upset but behaves with some dignity and accepts what she says.

Commentary This chapter consists entirely of the final conversation between Lucy and Cecil. It presents Lucy achieving her object – breaking up with Cecil – without admitting to him or to herself the real underlying reason. It is also an interesting completion of the character of Cecil who seems more likeable here than at any other point in the novel. Usually gleefully dogmatic and narrow in his thinking, he admits that he finds it difficult to interact with people. 'I am likely to say the wrong thing', he says with unexpectedly humble and accurate self-knowledge, and later admits: 'I have just used you as a peg for my silly notions of what a woman should be.' 'Bewildered' by Lucy's announcement, he gradually – sadly – notices that she is not the naïve young girl he thought he knew, but 'a different person: new thoughts – even a new voice' (p.181). At the last, we see beyond the caricature to a real person: 'By a cruel irony [Lucy] was drawing out all that was finest in his [Cecil's] disposition' as she breaks off their engagement (p.180).

Of course Lucy really does have a 'new voice' – her own inner voice – because she has listened to and absorbed (in spite of herself) what George had said earlier. She even quotes George's insights on Cecil's character to Cecil himself, while flatly denying that she is in love with someone else. Cecil accepts most of Lucy's criticisms and reasons that he is not fitted to be her husband, admitting that (as George had suggested) he is 'the sort that no one can know intimately'. One of the deepest ironies in this chapter – and indeed in *A Room with a View* as a whole – is that we see Lucy passionately declaring 'I won't be protected. I'll choose for myself what is ladylike and right' and 'I won't be stifled' as if speaking with a new voice. Yet if this is George's voice, is she even now expressing her own original thoughts and ideas?

At the end of the chapter, with heavy irony, Forster reminds the reader that Lucy has joined the ranks of people who deny 'passion and truth' because she has 'pretended to George that she did not love him, and pretended to Cecil that she loved no one else'.

Chapter 18: Lying to Mr Beebe, Mrs Honeychurch, Freddy and the Servants

Mr Beebe calls at Windy Corner, mainly to tell Lucy that he has had a letter from the Miss Alans who are planning a trip to Greece. On the way he sees Freddy taking Cecil to the station. Out of Cecil's hearing, Freddy tells Mr Beebe about the broken engagement. At the house Lucy plays Mozart while her mother and the others are gardening. Mr Beebe speaks to everyone and tells Lucy she has done the right thing. Mrs Honeychurch says that Lucy can go to Greece with the Miss Alans if she wishes.

Commentary Lucy continues to suppress her feelings, channelled initially into Mozart whom Mr Beebe (and Forster?) seem to regard as a second-rate composer compared with Beethoven. Lucy is 'tinkling at' a Mozart sonata Mr Beebe dismisses as a 'silly little [thing]' (p.189). (There is further discussion of the symbolism of Lucy's music on pages 65–6 of this study guide.)

Everyone close to Lucy is glad that she has dismissed Cecil. Mr Beebe is 'certain [she has] done the right thing', Mrs Honeychurch is 'thankful – simply thankful', just like Freddy. No one except Charlotte – from whom interestingly, we hear no direct comment other than the guardedly ambiguous 'It is always terrible when the promise of months is destroyed in a moment', apparently referring to the damaged dahlias – knows the real reason for Lucy's decision. These reactions suggest Forster is clarifying his modern view that at the dawn of the new century, a modern young woman needs the freedom to choose.

The letter from the Miss Alans conveniently presents Lucy – still in flight from her own inner feelings – with somewhere to run to. If she travels with them to Athens, Delphi and possibly Constantinople (now known as Istanbul) she will be a long way from Summer Street and the Emersons.

CRITICAL VIEW

The 'garden boy' (even Forster puts this in inverted commas) whom Minnie Beebe plays with is a reminder of the hierarchical social structure of Edwardian England. Young Lennie would have been required to do odd jobs in the garden at Windy Corner. A Marxist critic would note that Lennie's presence is a reminder of just how comfortably off Mr Honeychurch has left his family in an unequal capitalist society.

Chapter 19: Lying to Mr Emerson

Lucy and her mother visit the Miss Alans in London to confirm the travel arrangements for Greece. On the way home from the station they call at Mr Beebe's rectory to collect Charlotte who says she wants to attend a church service. Mrs Honeychurch goes with Charlotte while Lucy waits in the rectory, where she finds Mr Emerson. In conversation with him, Lucy at last admits that she loves George.

Context

Lucy suggests visiting Mudie's bookshop and lending library so that she can get a guidebook for her trip to Greece. Mudie's had started in 1840 in Upper King Street, Bloomsbury, but by the 1900s it had moved to bigger premises (now demolished) in New Oxford Street. Such references would resonate with Forster's readers.

Context

The Miss Alans are stereotypical Victorian-style spinsters who live comfortably enough on their unearned income not to have to work for a living. The temperance movement campaigned against the evils of alcohol and a 'temperance hotel' served nothing but soft drinks.

Commentary This chapter is the climax of the novel. The conversation with Mr Emerson is when everything finally and irrevocably changes. He 'managed to strengthen her. It was as if he made her see the whole of everything at once' (p.215). The fussy discussion with the Miss Alans which precedes it and the time spent in London with her mother clearly show Lucy's unrest and unease. She can't find a truthful way of explaining to her mother why she doesn't yet want her broken engagement made public – she is still trying to avoid George who might 'begin again' if he knew. She is 'drifting away from her mother' to such an extent that she tells Mrs Honeychurch that after Greece she might share a flat with another young woman in London rather than return to Windy Corner. She also squabbles tetchily with Mrs Honeychurch, who says she's beginning to behave like Charlotte. Forster uses all of this to convey Lucy's discontent and 'muddle' as she continues to try to suppress her true feelings.

> He [Mr Emerson] had robbed the body of its taint, the world's taunts of their sting; he had shown her [Lucy] the holiness of direct desire.

Top ten quotation

Build critical skills

It is possible to interpret Lucy's anger at her mother through a psychoanalytical critical lens here. In these terms, anger is often viewed not as a primary emotion, but as an outward projection of guilt, distress or fear. Underlying Lucy's anger, therefore, we might suspect there lies a core of unhappiness so intense that she feels an unconscious urge to mask it.

Forster builds much narrative tension into this chapter. The Emersons are leaving. The conversation between Mr Emerson and Lucy at the rectory seems like a chance encounter (although it isn't, in fact; Charlotte has stage-managed it) and

Build critical skills

The traditional Roman Catholic and Anglican religious belief is that new-born babies must be baptised as soon as possible to cleanse them from the 'original sin' they are born with. Without this ritual they will be unable to enter heaven and be condemned to purgatory for ever. The rational and enlightened Mr Emerson views this as absurd and refuses to have his son baptised. The vicar, Mr Eager, distresses the Emersons by referring to this decision as Mrs Emerson is on her deathbed. How do you respond to Forster's presentation of organised traditional religion here?

circumlocutions: roundabout and evasive ways of expressing things rather than getting straight to the point.

the Litany, the church service the others have gone to, is very brief. The reader infers that time is short for Mr Emerson and Lucy to get to get the point and indeed they are still talking when the others return and call for her. Mr Emerson is now quite unwell and waiting to move back to London to be with George. He tells Lucy that George is becoming depressed – he has 'gone under' (p.208). At last she learns what Mr Eager meant by his insinuations that Mr Emerson has 'murdered his wife in the sight of God' – he had refused to have George baptised, in accordance with his atheist, free-thinking, humanist views.

Lucy's initial efforts to maintain social conventions and 'remember how to behave' don't last long. Although she condemns George's actions (which Mr Emerson evidently knows about) as 'abominable', as soon as Mr Emerson hears that she is no longer engaged to marry Cecil he becomes impassioned. 'You love George!' he exclaims, and 'the three words burst against Lucy like waves from the open sea'. When she accuses Mr Emerson of being sexist in assuming that 'a woman is always thinking about a man', his direct and utterly accurate response is 'But you are' (p.212). He urges her, 'Then be his wife. He is already part of you' (p.212).

Mr Emerson drops the formal 'Miss Honeychurch' and begins to call her 'Lucy'. This is crucial, given the intimate and perceptive things Forster is having him say to her. He speaks, for example, of sexual arousal: 'that love is of the body, not the body, but of the body' (p.213). This free, full and frank conversation is a world away from the **circumlocutions** and evasions that surrounded Lucy in the earlier sections of the novel. The climax of the chapter occurs when Lucy has a momentous epiphany: 'the darkness was withdrawn, veil after veil and she saw to the bottom of her soul'. From this point on, as the narrator makes clear, she is going to marry George. The rest is mere detail.

▲ The British Museum, visited by Lucy and her mother in Chapter 19. The museum is in Bloomsbury where Forster had a flat near Virginia Woolf and others who came to be known as 'the Bloomsbury set'

This is one of the few times in the novel that we see Mr Beebe being less than pleasant and urbane. Not a fan of marriage at the best of times, he is 'grieved' to discover that Lucy has been misleading him. 'They have loved one another all along', says Mr Emerson. Dismissed quite offhandedly by Mr Beebe, Lucy turns back to Mr Emerson and sees 'the face of a saint who understood'. The word 'saint' is deeply ironic here, since Mr Beebe is an Anglican clergyman and Mr Emerson is an atheist and unbeliever.

Context

Forster presents Mr Eager as a glaring example of the smug traditionalist Anglican clergy accused by the woman's rights campaigner and preacher, Maude Royden-Shaw, of upholding an outrageously elitist social, political and cultural status quo. In a 1917 speech she famously challenged the Church of England to 'go forward along the path of progress and be no longer satisfied only to represent the Conservative Party at prayer'.

Chapter 20: The End of the Middle Ages

Exactly a year after the opening of the novel, Lucy and George are back in Florence at the Pension Bertolini enjoying their honeymoon in a room with a view. They discuss the events of recent months and realise that, unlikely as it seems, Charlotte Bartlett must have engineered that pivotal meeting between Lucy and Mr Emerson in the rectory by asking to go to the church service. In getting George's father and Lucy together, she helped to bring about the young couple's happiness.

Commentary Forster has used the word 'lying' in the titles of the previous four chapters to stress Lucy's refusal – even in her own mind – to face the truth. Since the end of Chapter 19 she has recognised the truth, struck out for independence and married George. This, Forster suggests, is enlightened modern behaviour which, in social and cultural terms, can be likened to the end of the middle ages and the beginning of the modern age.

The reader isn't given precise details of all the events of recent months but pieces together what must have happened through Lucy and George's conversation in this intimate bedroom scene. The servant is asked to leave them in honeymoon privacy and at one point they lie kissing on the bed; this is a strikingly modern scene that would have been frowned upon in a novel only a few years earlier, despite the fact that the protagonists are a respectably married couple. George's head lies in Lucy's lap, he carries her to the window and they 'whisper one another's names'. Their comfortable, relaxed, obviously sexual relationship is not hidden here. Lucy's sexual awakening is complete.

Christopher Booker has argued that all fiction is derived from one of seven stories. In *The Seven Basic Plots* (2004) he categorises these as Overcoming the Monster, Rags to Riches, the Quest, Voyage and Return, Comedy, Tragedy and Rebirth. Which elements of Booker's seven plots can you trace in *A Room with a View*?

All is not quite perfect. Lucy has married without her mother's blessing, telling the family that 'if mother wouldn't give her consent we should take the thing into our own hands'. This is what she means when she says she has 'alienated Windy Corner; perhaps for ever' (p.218). A clear blow for independence has been struck and Lucy is certain she has done the right thing – but she still wishes Cecil would not pontificate so much about women and that Mr Beebe 'did not influence them quite so much at Windy Corner' (p.218). However, one person has, rather surprisingly, played Cupid amid all the difficulties it seems. Lucy assumes that when she arrived at the rectory, had Charlotte known of Mr Emerson's presence, she 'would have stopped me going in, and I should have gone to silly Greece, and become different for ever'. However, George thinks very differently. He is certain that Charlotte knew very well that Mr Emerson was there, and thus she must have deliberately set up his meeting with Lucy. 'She is not withered up all through', says George, speculating that 'far down in her heart' Charlotte is glad that they are united at last.

Build critical skills

While the novel ends happily with Lucy and George together in the room which he gave up for her when they first met, the 2007 television adaptation by Andrew Davies added a poignant coda in which Lucy returns alone to Florence after George is killed during World War I. To what extent do you think it is justifiable to alter the original ending so drastically and what might Davies' reasons for doing so have been?

Target your thinking

- What are the key themes of *A Room with a View* and how does Forster develop them as the narrative progresses? (**AO1**)
- What narrative methods does Forster use to illustrate and explore his key themes? (**AO2**)

Love

The novelist and critic Zadie Smith suggests that:

Forster's folk are famously always in a muddle: they don't know what they want or how to get it. It has been noted before that this might be a deliberate ethical strategy, an expression of the belief that the true motivations of human agents are far from rational in character. Forster wanted his people to be in a muddle; his was a study of the emotional, erratic and unreasonable in human life.

(Smith, 2003)

'You don't mean that you're going to marry that man?' says George to Lucy of Cecil Vyse when he at last jolts her into beginning to think properly about her future (p.173). The love which George feels for Lucy and she for him, although she has yet to admit to herself, is based on feelings of heart and body. It is physical and emotional. '[L]ove is of the body; not the body, but of the body. Ah! The misery that would be saved it we confessed that,' Mr Emerson tells Lucy bluntly (p.213).

Taking it further ▷

In his short story *On the Western Circuit* (1891) Thomas Hardy writes of 'the belief of the British parent that a bad marriage with its aversions is better than free womanhood with all its interests, dignity and leisure'. Conversely Forster summarises Mr Beebe's view of marriage in *A Room with a View* as 'They that marry do well but they that refrain do better' (p.196). Consider both views of marriage with respect to *A Room with a View*.

On the other hand Lucy's 'love' for Cecil Vyse is convenient and conventional. It isn't based on physical attraction. Cecil's one chilly attempt to kiss her is a disaster – in comic contrast to both George's 'insults'. Whether Cecil is, as George suggests, a controlling man who 'daren't let a woman decide' (p.174) or not, he is, in the social environment Lucy inhabits, a suitable match for the heroine. Jane Austen makes the same point a century earlier in her pragmatic opening to *Mansfield Park* in which Miss Frances Ward 'marries to disoblige her family' and since her lieutenant of marines has no 'education, fortune or connections' she could hardly have made 'a more untoward choice'.

However, Forster can be interpreted as rather more romantic and less incisively pragmatic than Austen. He is presenting physical passion, mutual respect and a form of equality as an ideal basis for marriage. When George observes in Chapter 16 that Lucy should be allowed to decide for herself whether or not something shocks her, there is a hint that attitudes towards women are changing and that affects love and marriage. Finding herself alone in Florence in Chapter 5, Lucy finds it 'too dreadful not to know whether she was thinking right or wrong'. By Chapter 17 she is able to inform Cecil that she will think for herself 'what is ladylike and right' (p.181). Such a development is also an indication that her attitude to sexual love has changed too.

Forster gives Lucy feelings and ideas of her own which need to be nurtured by a lover such as George, not suppressed by a man like Cecil, 'the type who's kept Europe back for a thousand years' (p.174). The writer associates real love with the freedom to think and function as an individual as well as with passionate sexual desire — and it is desire, rather than a meeting of minds, which George and Lucy feel at first, because apart from after the street murder incident in Florence, they hardly speak to each other before their first passionate kiss. Note on that occasion that she feels she has 'crossed some spiritual boundary' and that 'wings seemed to flutter inside her' (p.44).

On the other hand, most of the older characters in *A Room with a View* are widowed, single or celibate. Forster uses the young Italian couple on the Fiesole jaunt in Chapter 6 to further develop his love theme. 'Phaeton' uses his job of driving the English to Fiesole as an excuse to take his girlfriend (nicknamed 'Persephone') out on a jaunt with him. Because they are peasants they are looked down upon by many in the English party; significantly their open physical affection for each other is frowned upon by Mr Eager and defended by Mr Emerson. They are drawn to each other physically and are happy to have found a way of spending the afternoon together. It's warm and natural. They are equals. Both are unconstrained. Although in the end the two are separated by Mr Eager, in a sense they are role models for Lucy and George who eventually follow suit by marrying and returning to Florence. Moreover, it's the cab driver, who clearly has freely expressed passions himself, who spots the chemistry between George and Lucy before either of them do. He directs Lucy to George among the violets because he is one of the 'good men'. She means the two clergymen in the party when she asks, and the cab man (deliberately?) misunderstands her.

Social class

Lucy's father was a successful solicitor who invested wisely, bought land and built a house in a developing part of Surrey. His money was earned not inherited (p.114). For this reason Mrs Honeychurch and her children don't behave like aristocrats.

They sing silly songs, tease each other, play tennis and are considerate to their servants. The Honeychurches are rooted in the 'best society obtainable' among people whose ideals are focused on 'kindly affluence, their inexplosive religion, their dislike of paper bags, orange peel and broken bottles' (p.114).

Because we are never told anything about the late Mr Vyse we are left to presume that Cecil and his mother are living on wealth passed down for generations. They look down on the Honeychurches who, for example, have modern furniture bought from shops rather than age-old family antiques. Mrs Honeychurch is well aware of this fact, as shown in her tart comment to Lucy: 'No doubt I am neither artistic, nor literary, nor intellectual, but I cannot help the drawing room furniture: your father bought it and we must put up with it, will Cecil kindly remember' (p.141).

Cecil regards it as his responsibility to 'educate' Lucy out of her 'vulgar' middle-class habits and attitudes, which include what he regards as a suburban obsession with 'Eggs, boilers, hydrangeas and maids' (p.147). Note though that the Vyses are not living in a grand stately home (although they are neighbours in Surrey) and Mrs Vyse seems to live mostly in a flat in London where Lucy visits her with Cecil in Chapter 11. Mrs Vyse's dinner party 'consisting entirely of the grandchildren of famous people' (p.126) is, Forster probably means us to observe, a rather strained way of keeping up class appearances while Lucy observes ruefully to herself that 'her London career would estrange her a little from all that she had loved in the past' (p.126).

Cecil – unlike George Emerson and Freddy – has no profession. As a Marxist critic might observe, people who had land and/or money did not have to work in order to eat. And the term 'working class' was originally a pejorative term for the vast majority of people who had to earn a living. By 1908, however, most people, regardless of social class, had some sort of profession. Mr Beebe certainly expects Cecil to have one, but Cecil comments languidly: 'I have no profession … My attitude – quite an indefensible one – is that so long as I am no trouble to anyone I have a right to do as I like' (p.94). Later Cecil sneers at people who write books for money. Forster himself had inherited enough money to free him from the necessity of working and was troubled by this; indeed he worked hard all his life and was never content to live on his inheritance. This may underpin his negative presentation of Cecil's attitude to work.

The Emersons are from a different social class again. Most of their money has to be earned – by Mr Emerson previously working as a journalist and by George now in a clerical position with a railway company. Both these positions clearly require intelligence and industry, although the snobbish upper-middle-class characters make snide remarks about George's being a member of the working class. Today some of the class attitudes expressed seem totally bizarre, such as when Charlotte is totally appalled by George's telling her that his profession is '"the railway". She was very sorry that she had asked him. She had no idea that it would be such a dreadful answer, or she would not have asked him.'

Taking it further ▶

Class and money in this novel must not be confused, as they are definitely not the same thing. You might enjoy comparing Forster's view of the English class system with Jane Austen's in *Pride and Prejudice*. There the class barrier is so strong that Lady Catherine de Bourgh famously accuses Elizabeth Bennet of having 'upstart pretensions' to join a social class for which she is totally unfitted as 'a young woman without family, connections, or fortune' by marrying her nephew Mr Darcy. Elizabeth rebuts Lady Catherine with: 'He is a gentleman; I am a gentleman's daughter,' she states; 'so far, we are equal.' He may be extremely rich and she may be rather poor, but even Lady Catherine is forced to admit the truth of this statement. How do the strengths of the class barriers compare in Forster's novel?

In the preface to his 1913 play *Pygmalion*, George Bernard Shaw declared it 'impossible for an Englishman to open his mouth without making some other Englishman hate or despise him'. You might enjoy comparing this witty comedy's presentation of the arcane British class system with that found in *A Room with a View*, given the texts were written just five years apart.

paternalistic: managing (and often limiting) the behaviour or freedom of an individual or social group rather as a very traditional father might exert control as the head of his family. It is a way of governing the behaviour of others in a manner which is suggested to be helpful and supportive, but can turn out to be oppressive and controlling.

The Emersons do not own a property and come to Summer Street to rent Cissie Villa which has a small garden in stark contrast to Windy Corner's thirty acres. Mr Emerson's marriage was 'advantageous' and they are not poor – like Lucy and Cecil, the Emersons have paid for a trip to Italy – but even so, almost every other character in the novel looks down on them. Cecil – who often berates Lucy for what he sees as her bourgeois social outlook – regards George as 'ill-bred' because he doesn't put on a jacket after tennis, to Forster's evident amusement.

The English social class system has long been complicated and finely nuanced, although by the early years of the twentieth century attitudes were beginning to blur largely because the nineteenth century had seen a huge growth in the prosperous middle classes and the development of suburbs around cities to accommodate them. That included people like Forster himself and his fictional Mr Honeychurch, a shadowy figure not unlike Forster's own architect father. Perceptions of, and attitudes to, social class permeate the text. The subtle gradations of snobbery can be seen in the Miss Alans, who see themselves as far more 'genteel' than Mr Emerson, making the mistake of thinking Cecil is not going to Greece with Lucy because he his detained in London by 'his work'. They haven't realised that Cecil is a 'gentleman who has a sufficient income not to have to work' (p.200).

The role of women

A critic exploring the novel from a feminist perspective might observe that all the characters in *A Room with a View* – male and female – regard women as inferior to men and in need of protection, apart from the Emersons and eventually Lucy herself. The novel is set in a **paternalistic** and **patriarchal** society against which some characters rebel. There are examples of this attitude on almost every page of the novel. Lucy has to be chaperoned in Florence by Charlotte and to Santa Croce by the unreliable Miss Lavish, for instance. Lucy believes for a long time that, in denial of her feelings, she must accept that Cecil is superior because he's a man and therefore the best person to guide her. Mr Beebe asks incredulously whether 'We are to raise ladies to our level?' (p.131). Mrs Honeychurch 'bothers over puddings' and can see no better prospect for Lucy than remaining at Windy Corner until marriage; she is scathing about girls who go to live in London with their 'typewriters and latchkeys' (p.203). Significantly she is very dismissive of the behaviour of campaigners for women's rights who 'agitate and scream' and are 'carried off kicking by the police' (p.203).

The Emersons, with whom Forster clearly sympathises, are different. Mr Emerson is widely read and thoughtful. He is a socialist who will have read John Stuart Mill, a very influential Victorian philosopher and thinker who argued passionately for women's rights. He recognises – long before she does herself – that what Lucy needs is friendship on equal terms within a sexual or married relationship, in direct contrast to Cecil, who has 'no glimpse of the comradeship after which the girl's soul yearned'. Mr Emerson uses the word 'comradeship' several times as an overarching summary of this sought-for gender equality when he speaks of 'the tenderness, and the comradeship and the poetry and the things that really matter' within a successful relationship (p.212). George has clearly inherited his father's views on equality; when he finally becomes impassioned and tells Lucy that she should be thinking independently, he also knows that Cecil 'daren't let a woman decide'. He offers her a clear choice between two sorts of relationships: Victorian or modern. When he tells her, 'I want you to have your own thoughts even when I hold you in my arms', it seems he is stating that he is an active supporter of the women's suffrage movement.

Lucy is, initially at least, no feminist in the modern sense but she does see things differently from her mother. She wants to think for herself even though she is frightened of her own feelings. The girl who in February is uneasy at being in Santa Croce without her Baedeker has by autumn 'developed since the spring'. With irony Forster tells us that he means she is now better able to 'stifle' her deepest feelings. In fact she has become more alert and more critical which is why she at last makes the sudden decision to part company with the controlling Cecil (p.176). '[H]e is so masterful. I found that he wouldn't let me go my own way. He would improve me in places where I can't be improved', she informs Mr Beebe (p.191). 'I will choose for myself what is ladylike and right. To shield me is an insult', she tells Cecil (p.181).

patriarchal: a patriarchal society is one in which men are afforded a uniquely privileged status. They are allocated dominant powerful roles in terms of politics, culture, morality and economics.

Context

Awareness of women's rights had been developing slowly for at least a century by the time Forster was writing. *A Vindication of the Rights of Woman* by Mary Wollstonecraft was published in 1792 for example. Both were seminal, influential works. Wollstonecraft was a pioneering feminist whose *Vindication* is the most influential early work of feminist philosophy. Attacking the dominant view at that time that women did not need training for anything beyond a limited domestic role, she argued that the education of women is essential so that they can raise their children well and be intelligent companions to their husbands. Wollstonecraft saw women as possessing the same fundamental and unalienable human rights as men.

Her position was seen as so radical that she was described by the essayist Horace Walpole as a 'hyena in a petticoat'. J.S. Mill's essay *The Subjection of Women* (1869), which was influenced by the ideas of his wife, Harriet Taylor Mill, was a passionately argued case for gender equality that was extremely radical for its time. Mill felt that the equality of the sexes would benefit men as well as women and as a Liberal MP, he consistently put forward the case for women's suffrage in the House of Commons. In this, he completely opposed the views of Queen Victoria herself, who was appalled by the idea of women having the vote.

A rebel she was, but not of the kind he understood – a rebel who desired, not a wider dwelling-room but equality beside the man she loved.

(p.115)

'Come this way immediately,' commanded Cecil, who always felt that he must lead women, though he knew not whither and protect them though he knew not against what.

(p.137)

Parents

Forster invites us to compare the relationship between Lucy (and to a lesser extent, Freddy) and their mother with the one between Mr Emerson and George. Also presented is the camaraderie between Cecil and his mother, and on the margins of the novel are Mr Beebe, with his mother and niece, to whom he is a quasi-father.

We first see Mrs Honeychurch as comfortable with Freddy while Lucy and Cecil are in the garden (Chapter 8). Lucy and her mother don't always agree. Mrs Honeychurch is uneasy about the marriage with Cecil but doesn't admit it until the engagement is broken off (pp.190 and 197). But later, perhaps 'disgusted at her [Lucy's] past hypocrisy' she doesn't give her consent to Lucy's marriage to George (p.218). An obvious interpretation is that Forster wants the reader to understand this as gentle but fairly traditional parenting by a woman who has no wish to embrace new ways of thinking. She is very dismissive of the growing trend of middle-class girls breaking free of family and trying to earn an independent living and clearly sees different futures for Freddy and Lucy because the former is male. There's a hint of this in the passing remark that Lucy used to swim naked in the pond with Freddy '… till I was found out, then there was a row.'

Although Mrs Honeychurch has a strong personality and runs her home efficiently (pp.85 and 145–7), on the whole she stands back and allows Lucy to do as she wishes, including the trip with Charlotte to Italy and the proposed trip to Greece with the Miss Alans. Mr Emerson, in contrast, makes no secret of George's being at the centre of his life – as his health deteriorates even during the year the novel covers. Mr Emerson desperately wants George to be happy, recognises from the beginning that Lucy and George are drawn to each other and, in his straightforward way, makes no secret of it: 'I don't require you to fall in love with my boy, but I do think you might try and understand him', he astonishes Lucy by telling her the morning after she has met them both for the first time (p.27). At the end of the novel, now not well enough to stay in Surrey and about to move back to London to be looked after by George, he tells Lucy that he is worried about his son who has 'gone under' (p.208) like his late mother. We are being shown a very involved, tender relationship – very different from the traditional, reserved father/son relationship usually associated with the middle and upper classes. There's even gentle warmth in the kindly image of George cleaning his father's boots on page 155.

Cecil and his mother are quite different. She speaks to him as an equal as if they are on a different side from Lucy who must somehow be brought over. 'Make Lucy one of us', she tells Cecil after hearing her play Schumann, noting approvingly that she is 'purging off the Honeychurch taint … not always quoting servants or asking how puddings are made' (p.127). We never see or hear

Mrs Vyse's reaction to the broken engagement but it's probably fair to assume that she would have been more distressed than Mrs Honeychurch: as Mrs Vyse considers Lucy to be Cecil's social inferior, for him to be jilted by a girl possessed of what they see as a bourgeois 'Honeychurch taint' would be a significant humiliation. All three parents, like almost all parents, want the best for their children but their approach to facilitating that varies.

Religion and Christianity

Forster, like most the Bloomsbury set and others he associated with, was a free-thinker and religious sceptic. Early on, he refers irreverently to 'papists' at Santa Croce, given to 'sousing each other with holy water and then proceeding to the Machiavelli memorial, dripping but hallowed' (p.21). No one in *A Room with a View* shows real religious commitment and a Christian critical standpoint might suggest that Forster is covertly mocking Christian belief. Mr Eager, formerly a clergyman in Brixton where the Emersons used to live and now in charge of the English Church in Florence, shows no Christian charity at all either to the Italian driver and his girl on the Fiesole trip or to the Emersons. The inference is that he and his type are rather loathsome. Gossipy tea-loving Mr Beebe is kinder but does not evince much spirituality in his dealings with parishioners. Through these clerics, Forster presents quite a cynical view of the Church of England which for Mrs Honeychurch and Charlotte is part of a respectable way of life rather than one dominated by belief. Note the fuss about clothes and money for the collection on pages 154–7 which reinforces the image of this attendance at church as a mere social obligation.

Mr Emerson is sceptical about religion and churches. He ridicules the mythology expressed in the frescoes (p.24) and is outraged at the way the church would have been built by poorly paid labourers. Later in the novel Forster asserts that Cecil admires 'honest orthodoxy' (p.157) but sneers at churchgoing for convention's sake. And he 'does not like parsons' (p.97).

Context

Jane Austen's novels are full of clergymen and, generally, she depicts them unflatteringly. While she does portray several good men of the Church, far more memorable and amusing are the snobbish, social-climbing Mr Elton in *Emma* and Mr Collins in *Pride and Prejudice*. Their arrogant and misguided proposals of marriage to Emma and Elizabeth respectively are scenes of great comic satire. Poking ironic fun at dodgy clerics is another link to explore between Forster and Austen.

Build critical skills

Fiction is full of bereaved children who have lost one or both of their parents, from Snow White to Harry Potter. In *The Uses of Enchantment* (1976), Bruno Bettelheim applies a psychological reading to various fairy tales, arguing that via their darker themes of violence, abuse, abandonment and death they allow children to externalise their deepest emotional fears and come to terms with them. Consider the missing parents in this novel – Mr Honeychurch, Mr Vyse and Mrs Emerson – and how Forster uses their absence as a plot device.

Context

England broke with Rome to become a Protestant country in the mid-sixteenth century and from then a sectarian distrust of Roman Catholic ritual and alleged 'superstition' was the norm for several centuries. The rational thinkers of the eighteenth-century Enlightenment tended to be anti-Catholic too. Mr Emerson's views appear to derive from this tradition. During the Victorian era, some influential churchmen based at Oxford University wanted to return to an older and more traditional faith. Two key members of the so-called 'Oxford Movement', John Henry Newman (1801-90) and Henry Edward Manning (1808-92), actually converted to Roman Catholicism and became cardinals.

The Catholic Church has always insisted on celibate – the word literally means unmarried – priests. After the Reformation priests in the new Church of England were permitted to marry but for a long time many of them did not. In Forster's time it was common for an Anglican priest like Mr Beebe to be celibate with a housekeeper to manage his household. Mr Eager appears to be unmarried too.

Today the meaning of the word celibate has shifted and it is usually taken to mean living without sex. Forster himself was unmarried but not celibate in the modern sense – there were casual affairs and some passionate friendships with men. Mr Beebe seems to recognise a kindred spirit in Cecil when he says that he thinks Cecil is, like him, not suited to marriage. Some critics might see this as a hint of homosexual leanings in both men.

In fact, almost all the characters in *A Room with a View* are living celibate lives either because they are widowed or single: Mrs Honeychurch, Mrs Vyse, Mr Emerson, Cecil, Mr Beebe, Charlotte – and even the Miss Alans and Mr Beebe's elderly mother. There are no married couples. Against this background the developing love between George and Lucy – which is physical, as well as of the mind, as Mr Emerson keeps observing – shines out dramatically.

Travel, art and culture

English people who don't need to work and can afford the cost have been travelling into mainland Europe for centuries – usually in search of art, music and experience of a different culture. Typically they went to Italy, the cradle of the Renaissance and famous for its priceless art treasures. The traditional rite of passage, known as 'The Grand Tour', saw the sons of the wealthy nobility travel abroad for many months or even years, collecting paintings to decorate the castles and stately homes they would in due course inherit; it might be thought of as a Georgian 'gap year'.

By the turn of the century, as we see in *A Room with a View*, tourism had become a little more democratic and the increasingly affluent middle classes were travelling too. Forster himself had travelled in Italy with his mother and modelled the Pension Bertolini on the Florence establishment they stayed in. At a deeper thematic level, however, *A Room with a View* is about Lucy's journey of self-discovery. A naïvely curious teenager when she first arrives in Florence, in just one year her experiences at home and abroad shape her emotionally, morally, psychologically and sexually. The novel's circular narrative finally returns the heroine to the same room with a view of the Arno that she slept in as an unmarried girl. When we leave Lucy, she is back at the Pension Bertolini as a mature adult, on her honeymoon with George.

Context

Travel is made easier for the characters in the novel due to the nineteenth-century expansion of the railways. Previous generations of tourists would have had to spend weeks stuffed into uncomfortable, horse-drawn carriages, but if Lucy and Charlotte travelled from London by train in 1908 they would have reached Florence in just a couple of days. The relative ease of the transport means it is not particularly odd for Lucy to consider going to Greece with the Miss Alans just three months after her return from Italy.

The range of references to paintings, books and music threaded through *A Room with a View* is vast and it is clear Forster expects his readers to be culturally literate enough to follow them. The art references are often symbolic and significant, underscoring an element of his characterisation or having a direct impact on the novel's action. A comic example of this is the extent to which Forster uses Cecil's consistent blunders to underscore what a sham he is. 'Occasionally he went wrong in a question of fact', we learn, before Forster has Cecil reveal his own ignorance by waffling about 'the Leonardo on the ceiling of the Sistine' (p.103). It is clear that Forster expects the reader to spot this rookie art history mistake; the ceiling of the Sistine Chapel in the Vatican in Rome was in fact painted by Michelangelo.

Lucy's piano-playing is another case in point. 'She was no longer either deferential or patronising: no longer either a rebel or a slave', notes the narrator. 'The kingdom of music is not the kingdom of this world: it will accept those whom breeding and intellect and culture have alike rejected' (p.30). Throughout the novel the reader is meant to be able to decode her musical choices along with her most analytical listener, Mr Beebe. When she plays a dramatic Beethoven piano sonata, Beebe is so overwhelmed by her passionate and intense performance that he stamps the ground in adulation and intuits that it is a signifier for Lucy's unconscious mind. Later, when she's trying to conceal

Build critical skills

A Marxist critical view might observe that travel is still mainly an option for people such as Lucy, Cecil and the Miss Alans, none of whom have jobs because of their independent income (apart from Charlotte, who is funded by Mrs Honeychurch). From a feminist viewpoint, it is also worth noting that while in the eighteenth and nineteenth centuries it was men only who made these trips, by the early twentieth century it has become acceptable for a young woman like Lucy to travel abroad, providing she is not alone.

TASK

The poet and critic T.S. Eliot coined the term 'objective correlative' to describe the way in which objects, situations or events can be used in literature to represent characters or emotions. Examine the ways in which Forster uses Lucy's piano-playing as an objective correlative for her altering states of mind throughout the novel.

▲ Creation of Adam on the Sistine Chapel ceiling

her complex feelings for Cecil and George even from herself, Lucy plays a rather more measured piece by Schumann, and even descends to 'tinkling' her way through Mozart in a way that Mr Beebe feels is beneath her. '[Lucy] entered a more solid world when she opened the piano.'

(See pages 65–6 for a more detailed discussion of this aspect and Forster's narrative style.)

In terms of literature, Cecil ridicules Miss Lavish's novel – but then we never see him reading for pleasure or have the chance to observe what he would actually choose to read. Effectively presented as a 'non-reader', therefore, Cecil's blinkered outlook seems unsurprising. The Emersons, of course, who are avid, intelligent and interested readers of an eclectic range of modern fiction and non-fiction, are seen to be open to new ideas and willing to learn.

Lucy is in Florence ostensibly to look at paintings – such as the Giottos in the church of Santa Croce – but she struggles to appreciate them and is gradually overtaken by real passion rather than the vicarious emotion suggested by looking at artworks. It is significant too that Mr Eager is lecturing a group of tourists, including the earnest, nervous Miss Alans, about the medieval Giottos created 'before any taint of the Renaissance' (p.24). It's a one-dimensional presentation which includes adjectives of excess such as 'majestic' and 'true' designed to reassure his audience but mean little in this context. Forster presumably intends that we should reflect on the dogmatic shallowness of a man who rejects the Renaissance as dangerously modern and realistic, preferring the simpler and more primitive works of Giotto.

Views

The word 'view' has two distinct meanings in English. It means a vista, such as the view of the Arno Lucy hankers for from her bedroom window in Florence. It also means an opinion or point of view. Mr Emerson, for example, is not interested in pretty views of scenery but he has strong views about love between a man and woman and socialist views about fairness and justice.

The views of many people in the novel – Cecil for instance and to a lesser extent Mrs Honeychurch and Mr Beebe – are very restricted. They can see only as far as the limited conventions of their way of life allow them to. Lucy needs, and wants, to break away from all that and to think – or see – independently so that she can make her own decisions and form her own views. She needs A Room with a View figuratively as well as literally (although it takes her a long time to realise it) and that's precisely what George gives her at the end of the novel when they are back together in the room which he relinquished for Lucy a year earlier.

A 'view' is about seeing. Some people in the novel can see very clearly indeed long before Lucy can. The cab driver whom Forster dubs Phaethon in Chapter 6 recognises the pull between Lucy and George and also that the Emersons are rather better people than either Mr Eager or Mr Beebe. He then deliberately misunderstands Lucy's question about the whereabouts of the '*buoni uomini*' (p.69), which leads to George's first impetuous, opportunistic kiss. Mr Emerson's view is highly accurate too. He spots the attraction between George and Lucy in Santa Croce in Chapter 2 although he doesn't articulate it fully until pages 209–15.

The physical titular room with a view becomes a symbol for the widening of Lucy's experience and the change in her circumstances over the course of the novel.

Charlotte is aware, although she can't really spell out why, that there is a danger in Lucy's acquiring a view from the Emersons which is why she tries so clumsily to refuse it at the beginning of the novel. She dwells pruriently on the horror of being told that Mr Emerson is taking a bath (p.12) and thinks it would be indecent for Lucy to occupy a room George has so recently had for his bedroom (p.13). Lucy innocently has the 'sense of larger and unsuspected issues' (p.13). Ironically, of course, Charlotte is right. Changing Lucy's view will, eventually, change everything. And the ultimate irony is that it is Charlotte herself who deliberately ensures that Lucy and George have a chance together (p.219). Even Charlotte has changed her view.

TASK

Make a list of Forster's mentions – with page numbers and notes – of the room with a view, from Chapter 1 onwards. Work out what he means with each mention.

Taking it further ▶▶

Search online for images of Giotto frescoes, painted about 1320 in the Peruzzi and Bardi chapels in Santa Croce. In 2010 art historians developed a technique using ultra-violet light to see past the centuries of deterioration and restoration to explore the detail of what Giotto actually painted. Consider what Mr Eager, who admires these works because 'they are untroubled by the snares of anatomy and perspective' (p.24), would think of this.

Target your thinking

- How does Forster develop his characters as the narrative progresses? (**AO1**)
- What narrative methods does Forster use to shape the readers' responses to the characters? (**AO2**)

Lucy Honeychurch

The novel's central protagonist is Lucy Honeychurch. Much of the third person narrative is presented from her point of view. She is the daughter of her successful solicitor father and lives with her widowed mother and brother among the 'best obtainable' (p.114) society in rural Surrey near Dorking. It is an area which is 'growing half suburban' (p.142). Socially she is a notch below the Vyses and several above the Emersons. Not a conventional heroine simply waiting passively for a fairy tale prince (like, say, Snow White or Cinderella), she has independent ideas and wants to think for herself. This is a tendency which worries Cecil, Mrs Honeychurch and Mr Beebe. In a married relationship Forster hints at 'the comradeship after which the girl's soul yearned' (p.161) as opposed to being merely protected, directed and controlled by any man she attaches herself to. Lucy also has sexual urges which she doesn't yet understand: 'his voice moved her deeply and she wished to remain near him' (p.148). Mr Beebe notices her passionate nature in the way she plays Beethoven. And Mrs Honeychurch is indirectly attributed with a dislike of music because it leaves her daughter 'peevish, unpractical and touchy' (p.41).

▲ Helena Bonham Carter as Lucy in the 1986 film

Lucy is on a journey of discovery about herself as the novel progresses. At the beginning she is merely looking for a mild, not particularly well-informed adventure in Florence. Her disquiet at George's presence and his kiss leads directly to the move to Rome, three months in Cecil's company and a rather reluctant agreement to marry him on their return to Surrey. She has already turned him down twice (p.86). The engagement to Cecil is presented as a temporary flight from her own 'muddled' feelings to a conventional position of safety. But there is no love – only tolerant affection – and no desire or passion. Then the 'scales fell from Lucy's eyes' (p.177) and Forster allows Lucy to proceed to the novel's inevitable (and conventional) conclusion – happy marriage. A critic examining this from a feminist perspective might note that, although Lucy seizes what she wants without family consent and marries George, she is still deferring to the patriarchal orthodoxy of marriage as the only allowable framework for such a relationship.

Taking it further ▶

A Room with a View is an early example of **modernist** fiction. Lucy is very different from, for example, the rather weak women in Dickens' novels such as Dora in *David Copperfield* (1850), always in need of protection. In many ways, Lucy is a new fictional woman for the new century and Forster is reacting against earlier trends. Gudrun in D.H. Lawrence's 1920 novel *Women in Love* is a free-thinking art school graduate back in her native mining town; the book was widely regarded as obscene at the time of its publication and takes the idea of an independent woman further. Virginia Woolf's *A Room of One's Own* (1929) became a classic of the feminist movement. Woolf argues, for example, that women need an independent income – and somewhere to live, and possibly work, privately to achieve equality with men.

Cecil Vyse

Cecil is a complex character who hides his vulnerabilities and social inadequacies (the failed kiss on p.112, for example) behind a veneer of assumed cultural superiority. He sneers and refuses to mix with the others – at tennis, for instance. He takes 'a malicious pleasure in thwarting people' (p.119). Mrs Honeychurch finds him rude (p.140) and George condemns him as fit only 'for society and cultivated talk', adding accurately that Cecil should 'know no one intimately, least of all a woman'.

But Forster does not allow Cecil to become a simply snobbish stereotype. In Chapter 17, when Lucy breaks the engagement, Cecil drops his posing and allows his distress to show through. He immediately develops into a much more likeable rounder character. He is humbler and much more honest. 'It is true', he declares in response to Lucy's assertion that he is not capable of an intellectually intimate relationship. 'I fell to pieces the day we were engaged' (p.181). Forster's humorous comment that 'nothing in his [Cecil's] love became him like the leaving of it' is as astute as it is unexpected. The reader is as surprised as Lucy is by Cecil's reaction to the jilting.

TASK

Read very closely the paragraph on page 21 which begins 'Then the pernicious charm...' and ends '...upturned toes'. When you have thought carefully about it, write a detailed, analytical commentary on this passage similar to the 'Extended commentaries' on page 93.

---

modernism: the term used to describe art of all genres which emerged between approximately 1900 and 1950. It refers to the breaking down of Victorian conventions such as linear storytelling and omniscient narrators.

Taking it further ▶

Take a close critical look at a character from another Edwardian novel where travel brings about a change for that character. Caroline Abbot in Forster's *Where Angels Fear to Tread* would make a good comparison with Lucy.

In plot terms Cecil has two main functions. He provides a means for Lucy to dabble with and then work out that she doesn't want a conventional marriage of convenience; he highlights by contrast everything which is attractive about George. Second, Forster has to find a way of bringing Lucy and the Emersons together once everyone is back in England and Cecil's malicious practical joke – perpetrated entirely by the snobbishness he so roundly condemns – is a neat device.

Taking it further ▶

Read Chapter 3 of Forster's *Aspects of the Novel*. Using Forster's terms, how would you categorise Charlotte and other characters in the novel such as Mr Eager, Freddy and Phaethon?

Build critical skills

In his 1927 book *Aspects of the Novel*, based on his lecture series at Trinity College Cambridge, Forster argues that all characters in novels are either flat or round. A 'flat' character, he says, is one who can be summarised in a single sentence. 'Round' characters are multi-dimensional and more complex. Decide how you would categorise Cecil Vyse who is, arguably, a fairly flat character until Chapter 17.

George Emerson

Initially presented as a rather reticent appendage to his forthright father, George Emerson gradually emerges during the course of the novel until he finally tells Lucy what he really thinks and feels at length on pages 174–5. Then it's like floodgates opening – an impassioned declaration for genuine human feeling based on honesty and lack of 'muddle' rather than shallow convention. Forster clearly means us to compare often quiet George with Cecil who voices loud opinions about almost everything. Even the two kisses which disconcert Lucy (and Charlotte) so much on pages 70 and 168 are snatched with silent spontaneous passion, in stark contrast with Cecil's talkative bungled effort on page 112.

George's outlook is completely different from Cecil's too. He works as a clerk for a railway company (p.153). He has been brought up by a socialist, atheist father who has also had to work for a living and isn't afraid to say what he thinks. Cecil, also apparently an only child, has grown up without the need to work, under the guidance of a mother who values material possessions (the 'well appointed flat' of Chapter 11) and dinner parties with the relations of famous people.

Forster uses George to make a point about education too. He and his father own an eclectic range of books (p.130) and both can quote from them. Cecil (like Forster) will have had an expensive – but probably quite narrowly focused – education in a top boarding school because that was the convention for men of his social class. George will have attended a different sort of school – one of the factors which makes him a conventionally unsuitable match for Lucy. And yet he is well-read and articulate and, in all the ways that matter to Forster, a better man than Cecil.

George's function in the novel is to be decent, honest and hardworking (Forster was critical of people who didn't work) and physically attractive enough ('Barefoot, bare-chested, radiant and personable', p.138) to arouse Lucy so that by the end of the novel her awakening is complete.

Mr Emerson

He's a character who arouses strong feelings in everyone he meets. Almost everyone at the Pension Bertolini in the early chapters is repelled by the lack of **obfuscation** (which he later refers to as 'muddle') in his manner. Polite society in 1908 relied on euphemism and circumvention. When Mr Emerson wants to offer his and George's room to Lucy and Charlotte he simply says so. And Charlotte notices a childishness in his eyes but realises it is not 'the childishness of senility' (p.4), the implication being that no one who is neither childish nor senile could or should behave like this. When Mr Emerson is reported to have offered a Miss Pole unsolicited advice about stomach acidity there is disquiet at his having mentioned a body part to a lady in public – which Forster presents humorously (p.36).

More seriously he speaks his mind at Santa Croce and infuriates Mr Eager with his socialism. At the end of the novel (pp.210–15) it is Mr Emerson whose lack of 'tact and manners' (p.9) or, to view it another way, whose straightforwardness, finally brings Lucy to her senses and makes her acknowledge what she feels for George. He is presented with great sympathy and sensitivity – an old man not in good health who relies on George to look after him – as the most perceptive character in the novel. Functioning rather like the chorus in a Greek drama, he comments wisely, for example, on the harmless (to the English travellers) relationship between 'Phaethon' and 'Persephone' (p.64). It is he who just before the end of the novel in Chapter 19 finally makes Lucy 'see the whole of everything all at once'.

He also has a secondary function of demonstrating how tender, kind and protective George is and that's part of the characterisation of both of them. George who 'hasn't learned to talk yet' (p.9) is well aware of how his father upsets people. 'My father has that effect on nearly everyone', he tells Lucy (p.25) after the contretemps with Mr Eager at Santa Croce.

Charlotte Bartlett

The archetypal poor relation, Lucy's older cousin Charlotte, 'whose travelling expenses were paid by Lucy's mother' (p.3), is her escort in Italy. Later, 'a prematurely aged martyr' (p.79), she comes to stay with the Honeychurches in Surrey because of plumbing problems at home in Tunbridge Wells. She has a comically irritating manner, frequently and tiresomely mentioning gratitude and status. Forster with restrained irony signals this with 'many a tactful allusion' on page 3. Forster refers to 'her wails' (p.151) and Mr Beebe thinks of her as one of the 'nervous old maids' (p.193) he is accustomed to dealing with.

She is an interestingly observed mixture of prudery, prurience and longing. She can't bear the idea of Lucy's occupying a room so recently occupied by George in Chapter 1 – or is she herself excited at the prospect of second-hand contact with an attractive young man? Much later in the novel she seems to concede 'far down in her mind' (p.220) that Lucy and George should have a chance together and is instrumental in Lucy having the chance of her life-changing

obfuscation: the process of making meaning so confused or opaque as to make it difficult to understand.

> **Build critical skills**
>
> An interesting piece of textual analysis would be to collect instances of Charlotte's prudery, prurience and longing and decide if any of them are viewed sympathetically either by Lucy or Forster.

conversation with Mr Emerson in Chapter 19. She is outwardly protective of Lucy but unreliable. She allows her to go to Santa Croce with the unreliable Eleanor Lavish whose flamboyance later seduces Charlotte into sharing inappropriate confidences – leading eventually to the inclusion of Lucy's experience with George among the Fiesole violets in Miss Lavish's third-rate novel. She feels unable to confront George a second time after the kiss in the rose garden at Windy Corner although, 'thoroughly frightened', she reluctantly agrees to be present while Lucy does so (pp.172/3). Significantly she hears George's impassioned declaration to Lucy and, completely unspoken, it evidently changed her opinion. 'Well it isn't everyone who could boast such a conquest, dearest, is it?' (p.176) she comments roguishly when she and Lucy pretend to each other that nothing significant has happened.

> 'I always said he was a cad, Dear. Give me credit for that, at all events. From the very first moment – when he said his father was having a bath.'
>
> (Charlotte to Lucy, p.171)

She's a character the reader might feel sorry for. She's single (and a feminist critic would probably say sexually frustrated, which would account for the overreaction, by modern standards, to George's 'assaults' on Lucy) and has very little in her life to make her happy. She is well aware that Lucy finds her intensely irritating. So does Mrs Honeychurch, who when she's really annoyed with Lucy tells her daughter that she is beginning to behave like Charlotte (p.203).

Forster uses Charlotte as a way of hooking his plot together. It is while staying at Charlotte's home in Tunbridge Wells that Lucy first met Mr Beebe – now in Florence on holiday and about to become Rector of Summer Street.

> Happy Charlotte, who though greatly troubled over things that did not matter, seemed oblivious to the things that did.
>
> (p.57)

The incident in which Charlotte arrives at Windy Corner, not by the agreed arrangement, and makes a tedious business of paying her own cab fare is as fine a piece of comedy as anything in the novel. Cecil, Freddy and Lucy become ever more exasperated but nervous Charlotte simply can't stop (pp.149–51). Note though that as soon as Charlotte finds herself alone with Lucy she drops it and reverts quite incisively to George and asks 'quite briskly' (p.151) for an update on what Lucy has, or has not, told Cecil.

Context

Charlotte Bartlett comes from a nineteenth-century literary tradition of genteel but poor maiden or widowed aunts, sisters and cousins. Mrs Norris in Jane Austen's *Mansfield Park* is a good example although she is much more comically vindictive and unpleasant than Charlotte. Brontë's Jane Eyre is the poor cousin of the Reed family. As the novel is a first person narrative, the reader is led to sympathise more with Jane's situation than with Charlotte's. In Trollope's *Barchester Towers*, Mary Bold lives with her wealthy sister-in-law but she is bright and cheerful and there is no suggestion of poverty or dependence. Her position is closer to what Lucy's would have been, had she gone abroad as the Miss Alans' companion.

Mr Beebe

An Anglican clergyman, Arthur Beebe is the new Rector at Summer Street and thus the Honeychurch family's parish priest. Lucy has met him at Tunbridge Wells in the past and at the beginning of the novel in Florence. He is a lifelong bachelor, responsible for his elderly mother and (partly) for his niece Minnie who spends much of her time at Windy Corner.

He has a camaraderie with other men – the comic scene in which he bathes naked with Freddy and George in Chapter 12 epitomises it. Generally, although he's outwardly kind, courteous and tactful ('adept at relieving situations'), he isn't much in favour of marriage. This is a man who has a 'belief in celibacy so reticent, so carefully concealed beneath his tolerance and culture' (p.196). Forster mentions the 'bitter disappointment which he could not keep out of his voice' (p.96) when Cecil initially tells him of his engagement to Lucy. Later he wants to help Lucy 'confirm her resolution of virginity' (p.196). There are at least two possible interpretations here. Either Mr Beebe admires Lucy's independent-spirited passion so much that he regards her throwing herself away on Cecil as very regrettable, or he dislikes the concept of marriage so much for himself that he is always disappointed to hear of anyone embarking on it. At the end of the novel Lucy, who is aware of his attitude, observes of Mr Beebe that 'he will never be interested in us again' adding sadly 'I wish that he did not influence them so much at Windy Corner'.

Much of the commentary about Lucy's playing is presented through Mr Beebe, from his reaction to her Beethoven (p.31) to her 'tinkling at a Mozart sonata' (pp.187 and 189). He is presented as a very cultured man, clearly very knowledgeable about music in a way that neither George nor Cecil is. Mr Beebe is, one presumes, more like Forster himself who evidently expects his reader to understand the allusions.

Forster often uses Mr Beebe as a way of linking characters and actions. It is he, for example, who liaises between the Emersons and Charlotte and Lucy at the Pension Bertolini so that they get their rooms with views. And it is in his rectory that Lucy has her all-important conversation with Mr Emerson in Chapter 19.

He is not a straightforward character though. Kind – to the Emersons for example – on the surface, his thoughts are as snobbish as Cecil's or the other guests at the pension.

▲ Mark Williams as Mr Beebe in the 2007 TV adaptation

> Mr Beebe, though unreliable, was a man of parts.
>
> (p.61)

> He [Mr Beebe] said: 'Oh he's [Cecil's] like me – better detached. Since Cecil's come after Lucy he hasn't been so pleasant – I can't explain.'
>
> (Freddy to Mrs Honeychurch, p.88)

CRITICAL VIEW

Karl Marx argued that religion is the opium of the people – a human invention created to anaesthetise people – and a Marxist critic might note that Mr Beebe seems to spend very little time doing what the Church of England pays him to do. There are only two references to his taking services: the one attended by Mrs Honeychurch, Charlotte, Lucy and Minnie in Chapter 15 and the Litany on page 205. Otherwise he seems to cycle round the parish in search of tea at the homes of his parishioners. See pages 93 and 98, for example.

Marian Honeychurch

Lucy's widowed mother is a fairly stereotypical mother of her time. She dislikes change (p.189), thinks Lucy should remain at Windy Corner until marriage to a suitable man and is very dismissive of the campaigns for women's suffrage (p.203). On the other hand, she's playful with Freddy when we first 'meet' her in Chapter 8 and kind. She invites Charlotte to stay and she helps to look after Minnie Beebe. Not as disdainful as Mrs Vyse and Cecil would like her to be, she does some cooking and gardening herself and is considerate to the servants. Although she is 'simply thankful' (p.197) when Lucy ends the engagement to rude, pretentious Cecil she is, the reader might infer from Lucy's conversation with George at the end of the novel (p.218), not willing to agree to Lucy's marriage to George — partly because George is deemed unsuitable and partly because she has concluded that Lucy's jilting of Cecil was the result of falling in love with George.

Cuthbert Eager

Mr Eager is the clergyman in charge of the English church in Florence. Formerly he ran the parish in Brixton where the Emersons once lived. He is presented as unpleasantly dogmatic with few, if any, redeeming Christian virtues. He insists that Mr Emerson's refusal to have George baptised caused the death of Mrs Emerson by divine punishment (pp.55/6 and 208). He treats 'Phaethon' and 'Persephone' with unnecessary unkindness on the Fiesole trip.

Freddy Honeychurch

Lucy's younger brother is studying to be a doctor — hence anatomy books and bones (p.85) lying about in the drawing room at Windy Corner. He is affable, friendly, kind (playing games with Minnie Beebe, page 116/7) and likes humorous songs but is disconcerted by Cecil who makes him feel inferior. Freddy doesn't read much apart from his medical textbooks (p.130). He invites George to bathe and later to play tennis at Windy Corner which brings him and Lucy back into proximity.

Eleanor Lavish

Miss Lavish is a rakish author of racy fiction. 'We literary hacks are shameless creatures', she says, with truth, on page 49. She smokes with the men and strides round Florence alone saying mildly shocking things. She befriends Charlotte who is so flattered by the attention of someone so exotic that she takes her eyes off Lucy at Fiesole. Charlotte also confides in the 'unreliable' Miss Lavish, which means that George's first kiss gets into her novel, something Cecil delights in ridiculing without knowing its provenance. Although she's no literary writer, Miss Lavish is interesting because she is independent and not succumbing to male domination. In making her seem laughable, Forster may be belittling her freedom of thought, however. He does not allow Lucy to emulate her.

Minnie Beebe

Minnie is Mr Beebe's thirteen-year-old niece. Her function in the novel seems to be to give Lucy and Freddy – both still very young, in contrast to Cecil who behaves like a middle-aged man – the opportunity to show playfulness and to provide a reason for Mr Beebe and Charlotte to go out to tea together in Chapter 18.

Writer's methods: Form, structure and language

Target your thinking

- How does Forster develop his themes, settings and characters? (**AO1**)
- What narrative methods does Forster use to shape the reader's response as the story unfolds? (**AO2**)

Form and genre

One genre that we might see reflected in *A Room with a View* is that of the traditional Bildungsroman (from the German meaning 'a novel of formation or education'), in which the narrative traces the development of the central character from childhood to adulthood. Sometimes called a 'coming of age' novel, the ways in which the main protagonist grows and matures is the backbone of the story. While the time span of *A Room with a View* is just a year, the bones of the genre are traceable in the novel's focus on the moral and psychological development of Lucy Honeychurch.

The central character in *A Room with a View* is a sensitive person who learns about life as she gains experience of the world, which is totally in line with the parameters of the genre. In the traditional Bildungsroman, this search for knowledge and understanding involves a trace of the old fairy tale trope of the young hero who leaves home to seek his fortune – and Lucy's journey to Italy fulfils many of these functions. The novel ends when the central character has literally and metaphorically grown up and reached the end of their quest for enlightenment and understanding. Significantly this desirable state is not achieved easily; often the protagonist comes into conflict with the norms and values of their society and takes many false steps along the pathway to maturity. Again, despite the shortened timescale, *A Room with a View* is significantly aligned with this generic structure.

Perhaps it seems odd to consider *A Room with a View* as a coming of age novel before looking at it as a love story, which is the genre within which it is most commonly situated. Yet seeing the text as primarily a 'light and bright and sparkling' comic romance, which is how Jane Austen described her most enduringly popular novel *Pride and Prejudice*, might have sat rather uneasily with E.M. Forster himself, as the novelist and critic Zadie Smith has pointed out.

Smith notes that while Forster knew *A Room with a View* was, in his own words, 'clear, bright and well constructed', it was in fact this very clarity and simplicity that bothered him. The ease of the read, the vivid characterisation, the satisfactory patterning of the plot – in short, all the things that lend the novel its pleasurable aspect – felt like failures to him. In a letter to his friend

Taking it further ▶

Perhaps the classic Victorian example of the female-centred Bildungsroman is Charlotte Brontë's *Jane Eyre* (1847), which traces the heroine's life from being a neglected and unwelcome ten-year-old orphan living with her callous aunt and cousins to her eventual happy marriage and the birth of her first child in her early twenties. Given that *Jane Eyre* covers at least a decade, unlike *A Room with a View*'s single year, you might compare the different ways in which Brontë and Forster work with the coming of age novel.

R.C. Trevelyan on 11 June, 1907, Forster expresses his concern with the novel, whose long gestation period had yet brought it no other name but *Lucy*: 'I have been looking at the "Lucy" novel. I don't know. It's bright and merry and I like the story. Yet I wouldn't and couldn't finish it in the same style. I'm rather depressed. The question is akin to morality.' This is where positioning *A Room with a View* within the Bildungsroman genre may shed light upon Forster's wider concerns.

Zadie Smith argues that he wanted to write something more than a sunny love story; instead, she suggests, he wished to explore the notion of what he calls in his letters and diaries the 'undeveloped heart'. Defining an 'undeveloped heart' as one that 'makes its owner march to their destiny by catchwords', living not by their own feelings but by the received ideas of others, Smith suggests that the characters in *A Room with a View* can be differentiated by the extent to which their hearts develop during the course of the novel. So while Lucy's heart grows, 'Charlotte Bartlett's will never develop through neglect and Cecil Vyse's is condemned by ill use' (Smith, 2003). Smith values Forster's attempt to show us 'how very difficult an educated heart is to achieve. It is Forster who shows us how hard it is to will oneself into a meaningful relationship with the world; it is Forster who lends his empathy to those who fail to do so' (Smith, 2003). Ironically, of course, in terms of the 'coming of age' genre, which is usually about acquiring knowledge and experience of the world, this almost happens in reverse for Lucy, as Smith argues further:

> It is not by knowing more that Lucy comes to understand, but by knowing considerably less. She starts off very certain, and in her certainty she lies to George, she lies to Mr Beebe, to her mother, to her brother Freddy and the servants. She tells all of them that she is certain of her own heart and mind. But it is by a process of growing less 'certain', less consistent, less morally enthusiastic, that she moves closer to the good she is barely aware of desiring.
>
> (Smith, 2003)

In her struggle to achieve the emotional and spiritual freedom of the 'developed heart', Lucy Honeychurch's story can indeed be seen as a kind of Bildungsroman.

Romance or love story

One of the commonest narrative tropes in all fiction is the separation of true lovers. In Shakespeare's *Romeo and Juliet*, of course, the feud between the rival Montague and Capulet families prevents the 'star-cross'd' lovers from having a future together and leads directly to tragedy. Yet barriers to love need not be permanent; *A Room with a View* is a love story in which there is, of course, a happy ending. As with Jane Austen's archetypal comic romance *Pride and Prejudice*, the love between Lucy and George is threatened by class prejudice and snobbery. For most of the novel Lucy's upbringing conditions her into rejecting George and agreeing to marry Cecil. But the novel closes with a modernised fairy tale ending which takes the reader beyond the assumption that 'they lived happily ever after'. It provides a scene with George and Lucy in their room with a view enjoying their honeymoon. Their relaxed teasing suggests that they are indeed a perfect match, destined for long-term happiness based on mutual respect and sexual equality.

A Room with a View is clearly a romance; Forster explores strong feelings of love that would not be out of place in a text from the high point of Romanticism. Yet he does so in an age of modernism, at the dawn of a new century, and puts a new twist on the genre by combining it with a sharp social critique. It is well worth remembering that the word 'romantic' is linked to the French word *romance* (story) and implies a search for meaning and identity; Lucy Honeychurch finds *herself* as much as her 'handsome prince' at the end of this modernist fairy story.

CRITICAL VIEW

Seen through a feminist critical lens, the life that might have been Lucy's had she married Cecil and come under the influence of Mrs Vyse is that of the stereotypical submissive 'Angel in the House' immortalised in Coventry Patmore's famous Victorian poem. Indeed her expected role is encapsulated in the line, 'Man must be pleased; but him to please / Is woman's pleasure'. Search online for this poem, and see if you can find any other phrases or ideas which reflect the idealised wifely role that Lucy rejects.

Context

Romanticism was a European cultural phenomenon encompassing not only all literary forms but also art, music, politics, philosophy, science and religion. Spanning the time period c.1770–1840, Romanticism was set against a historical background of radical change that included the American and French Revolutions. Traditional beliefs were questioned, challenged and reinterpreted. The established Enlightenment ideals of logical, systematic, scientific rationalism gave way to an exciting, unstable age. Lucy's musical hero, Ludwig van Beethoven, was a leading Romantic composer and therefore her identification with his art is symbolic and significant.

Seen through the critical lens of feminism, the classic wedding which is a staple ending of so much classic romantic fiction sees a young woman step into an unknown world in which she surrenders control over her future life to her husband. Forster, it could be argued, is consciously acknowledging Lucy as an autonomous individual by showing her after her marriage. That comfortable intimacy between Lucy and George, with kneeling on the floor, kissing her, accepting her teasing, and lying on the bed with her chatting in the room they share at the Pension Bertolini evokes a strong sense of the passionate sexual relationship between equals. The great Victorian novelists were unable to take their readers beyond the bedroom door. In the end, while Lucy is caught between the social, sexual and cultural respectabilities of the old century and the emergent yearnings of her 'undeveloped heart' at the dawn of the new one, the battle is ultimately successful.

Comedy of manners

A Room with a View can be seen as a romantic comedy, even though this term is more often applied to plays rather than novels. The reader enjoys a relaxed superiority over the characters (we know what's happening to Lucy long before she does.) And the novel, with its extensive use of irony, is quite often amusing. But the comedy of manners genre amuses us by satirically poking fun at the habits and affectations of a particular social class – in this case the English middle class.

Context

Written just 13 years before *A Room with a View*, Oscar Wilde's *The Importance of Being Earnest* (1895) is perhaps the most famous of all English stage romantic comedies. It features the tribulations of young lovers, exactly as Forster's novel does, but in a comically topsy-turvy and farcical form.

The comedy of manners genre is famous for its use of instantly recognisable stock characters – archetypes that occur time and time again in this specific literary context. Stock characters are easily parodied and offer plenty of scope for creating comedy; thus when Cecil Vyse is mocked for his pretentious boasting, Forster is making use of him as a classic 'fop' or upper-class fool. Another good example of this typical comedy of manners technique can be seen during the visit to Fiesole in Chapter 6, when Charlotte fusses about so irritatingly about not needing to sit on a waterproof square. Here Forster casts her as a fussy old maid reminiscent of Jane Austen's Miss Bates in *Emma* in a pitch-perfect comic set-piece. Even Lucy Honeychurch, usually presented as a fully rounded character, exhibits signs of being a classic damsel in distress when she has to be rescued during the street murder scene by George Emerson, who functions at this point as a stock Byronic hero, enigmatic, powerful and misunderstood.

Context

The trope of the eternal triangle is a staple within romantic fiction, providing rich opportunities for a writer to explore the darker side of human relationships where adultery, jealousy and pain coexist. In *A Room with a View*, of course, the trope plays out comically, as Cecil is defeated by Lucy's love for George.

Build critical skills

As you consider the form and genre of the novel, bear in mind that Forster has embedded a writer of romance fiction within his text in Eleanor Lavish in what may be seen as an early experiment in metafiction. Moreover, he pokes fun at the prudish sensibilities of the stereotypical 'ladylike' Victorian reader through his presentation of Charlotte Bartlett. His pointed social satire has Charlotte appalled by the mere mention of a man's stomach in polite company but revelling in Miss Lavish's raciness.

Structure

Consider the structure of a text as the means and manner in which it is built. At A-level you need to understand the ways in which the structural aspects of a literary work contribute to and influence our understanding of the text as a whole. There are some key structural devices used by Forster which you should study in detail.

The time span of one year: Linear chronological movement

Taking it further ▶

Forster's decision to filter the narrative almost always through his heroine is reminiscent of the way Jane Austen chooses to tell her stories of love and romance. You might enjoy comparing Forster's presentation of Lucy Honeychurch with Austen's portrayal of Elizabeth Bennet in *Pride and Prejudice*, as both heroines are flawed but thoroughly likeable and often get themselves into a fine romantic mess before the eventual 'happy ending'.

A Room with a View is told chronologically as a third person narrative, with Lucy almost always functioning as the narrative centre of consciousness. It opens in February in the city of Florence and ends there almost exactly a year later. Its 20 chapters are split across the two parts of the novel. Part One – about the first third of the novel – ends at the end of Chapter 7 when Lucy and Charlotte leave Florence. The remaining 13 chapters from Part Two and the rest of the narrative are almost entirely set in England.

Occasionally there are brief flashbacks such as at the opening of Chapter 10, which fills in the back story of Lucy's father and why she and her family are in their current situation. Generally though, Forster moves from one event to the next in a linear fashion while filling in key information retrospectively. Thus we see Lucy and Charlotte leaving Florence at the end of Chapter 7 (and Part One) and, as Part Two opens, we find her back at home in Surrey in August accepting a proposal of marriage from Cecil. Three or more months have passed and Forster patches in brief references about this 'missing' time spent in Rome. We learn, for instance, that Cecil has proposed to Lucy twice before, presumably in Rome. Similarly the narrative shifts from Lucy's conversation with Mr Emerson at the end of Chapter 19 to her on honeymoon with George in Chapter 20. Months have passed and Forster isn't interested in the minutiae of how she and George came together, resisted the objections of her family and married – all of this is mentioned only in retrospect in the dialogue in Chapter 20.

The underpinning narrative arc: Lucy and George's developing love story

The love story between Lucy and George hangs on six main events and incidents which form the narrative spine of the novel. You should re-read these key episodes closely and make notes on them. Notice that they are surprising but significant brief interludes that stand out against the backdrop of the rest of the novel:

❐ The first meeting at the Pension Bertolini in Florence (pp.4–7)

❐ The kiss at Fiesole (p.70)

❐ The kiss at Windy Corner (p.168)

❐ George's declaration of love (pp.174/5)

- Lucy's conversation with Mr Emerson (pp.208/15)
- The honeymoon at the Pension Bertolini in Florence (pp.216–19)

Linking together these moments in time are other developments, comments, observations and comic set-pieces, but at the heart of *A Room with a View* is a chronologically ordered linear story moving from Florence to England and back again to Florence and the final uniting of the two young lovers.

Binary opposites, juxtapositioning, patterning and doubling

The concept of binary opposites stems from the work of the French intellectuals Claude Lévi-Strauss (1908–2009) and Roland Barthes (1915–80), who were closely associated with the theory of **structuralism.**

In terms of literary theory, structuralists argue that since the meaning of a word is not actually contained in its name, we tend to construct its meaning by relating each word to its opposite. They characterise words as symbols which signify society's ideas and suggest meaning emerges from the gap between two opposing concepts; thus in order to grasp an idea such as *masculinity* we refer to its binary opposite *femininity*. Layers of inferential meaning can emerge when a writer consciously structures a text using core oppositions and patterns like this, and in *A Room with a View* Forster makes frequent use of this technique by inviting the reader to consider such essential **dichotomies** as:

- masculinity and femininity
- passion and celibacy
- rebellion and conformity
- present and past
- fertility and sterility.

Inviting the reader to consider similar or contrasting ideas or concepts can shed light on them both. Think about Forster's reasons for using the structural techniques of juxtapositioning, patterning, doubling and/or foreshadowing in the following examples:

- England and Italy
- Lucy and Charlotte
- Lucy's romantic encounters with George and Cecil
- Mr Beebe and Mr Eager as benevolent and malevolent clerics
- Mrs Honeychurch and Mrs Vyse as mothers
- Mr Eager and Mr Emerson as cleric and atheist
- Charlotte and Mr Emerson as 'cupids'; this unlikely pair of opposites help to unite George and Lucy. Mr Emerson, of course, does this overtly and boldly due to his love for his son, whereas Charlotte's intervention is both unexpected and extremely discreet.

structuralism: the search for the underlying patterns of thought in all aspects of human life, involving the comparison of the relationships between elements in any given system.

dichotomy: a division into two mutually exclusive, wholly separate parts.

Chapter headings

picaresque: a text that tells of the exploits of a lovable rogue (like Tom Jones himself).

The novel's 20 chapters each have a heading, like many much earlier classic texts. Henry Fielding (1707–54) famously did it in his **picaresque** comic rollercoaster *Tom Jones*. Charles Dickens (1812–70) and Anthony Trollope (1815–82) both made extensive use of chapter headings, although Jane Austen (1775–1817) simply numbered her chapters so the decision has always been a matter of personal taste. In general, however, the practice was going out of fashion by the early twentieth century, so Forster's deliberately archaic and quirky chapter headings seem to be sending up the habits of his literary predecessors. The fact that they are listed at the front of the novel as a table of contents means that the reader is faced with an enigmatic synopsis of the novel even before he or she turns to the first page.

Traditionally chapter headings fulfil a number of functions and Forster's adoption of various different styles shows his fond imitation – or satirical mockery – of his forebears. Some headings simply summarise the contents of the chapter: Chapter 7, 'They Return', being a case in point – and yet even this is a lightly mocking understatement, given that this chapter shows us the aftermath of Lucy and George's first kiss. Other headings indicate setting, although they too can be tinged with ironic humour: Chapter 11 is labelled so that the reader knows the scene about to unfold is to take place 'In Mrs Vyse's Well-Appointed Flat'. Of course the narrative focus of the chapter is not Mrs Vyse's interior decoration; what follows this tongue-in-cheek heading is an analysis of the problematic developing relationship between Lucy and Cecil. Thus Forster's titles can appear to focus on a trivial trigger point or detail which is almost beside the point. In pretending that Mrs Vyse's flat is the crux of the chapter, he plays the classic card sharp's trick of momentarily distracting our attention. It is in the notable gap between what the writer declares is the chapter's focus and what's really of central narrative importance that a rich vein of dry humour can be found. It also serves to remind us of the rigid Edwardian social codes of politeness and manners that for so long prevent the real truth being confronted in the novel.

Again, the heading of Chapter 6 – 'The Reverend Arthur Beebe, the Reverend Cuthbert Eager, Mr Emerson, Mr George Emerson, Miss Eleanor Lavish, Miss Charlotte Bartlett and Miss Lucy Honeychurch Drive Out in Carriages to See a View; Italians Drive Them' – is very long and clumsy, in direct mimicry of Henry Fielding's long, rambling titles for the chapters of *Tom Jones*. The point of it is that the seven people listed were together and that significant things develop between them. The carriages, the view (both from the hilltop and in the sense of opinion) and the Italians all affect the events of the day. Only once you have read the chapter does the heading make sense.

Forster also uses his chapter headings to act as a running commentary on the action. For most of the novel Lucy is deep in self-delusion. Much of what she says and thinks is therefore not the truth. Chapters 16, 17, 18 and 19 all have 'lying' in the title. Lucy lies to everyone because she isn't yet ready to face the truth within herself. Yet the significant facts – that firstly, Lucy doesn't realise she's lying to all these people and, secondly, that she is, of course, most of all lying to *herself* – are stressed through this repetitive chain of chapter headings.

The chapter after Lucy's return to Italy (Chapter 8) is called 'Medieval'. In this chapter she takes a step backwards by agreeing to marry Cecil, rejecting independence and rational thinking. If this were the history of Western thought she'd be back in the superstitious Middle Ages, Forster suggests, before the coming of the eighteenth century with its Age of Enlightenment. This is comparable with what happens to Lucy – hence Forster's calling the final chapter 'The End of the Middle Ages'. At other times, of course, Forster humorously satirises the whole concept of inventing appropriate (or sometimes, as we have seen, deliberately inappropriate) chapter headings by simply refusing to do it. Thus Chapter 4 and Chapter 12 are simply headed 'Fourth Chapter' and 'Twelfth Chapter'.

The omniscient narrator and the implied audience

Forster's third person style features an omniscient narrator – an all-knowing, invisible God-like being who knows everything about the story and can present an overview of it all as if present at every event. Good examples of this include the conversation that takes place between Mrs Honeychurch and Freddy in Chapter 8 and that between Mrs Vyse and Cecil in Chapter 11; although Lucy is the novel's central protagonist, Forster informs the reader of things that happen when she isn't there and thus cannot report on. Yet the all-seeing narrator can be selective, choosing to withhold his opinion and remain focused in one place while something perhaps equally interesting is happening elsewhere – something that the reader has to accept they will never know about. Thus while Freddy and Mrs Honeychurch are chatting together in the drawing room, Cecil is in the garden proposing to Lucy; rather maddeningly the omniscient narrator decides to stay with the heroine's brother and mother, so the reader finds out no more about Cecil's proposal than Freddy and his mother do. How do we let the storyteller get away with this? Because, in the end, we want to. The reader's acceptance of the narrator's authority is part of that willing suspension of disbelief that enables us to fully enter the world of the novel.

In trusting *A Room with a View*'s invisible narrator and accepting what he or she chooses to tell us, of course, we are reading the text very differently to the way in which we would a first person narrative in which the character telling their own story is often made deliberately biased, partial and unreliable to create a sense of uncertainty and instability. Forster is having none of this, following the traditional pathway of the novelist-as-puppeteer, pulling the strings of his characters (and arguably his readers too). He stands behind his characters and makes them do and say whatever he wants.

Jane Austen famously interpolated what seem to be directly personal views into her otherwise omniscient narratives. 'Let other pens dwell on guilt and misery', she declares towards the end of *Mansfield Park* (1814). 'I quit such odious subjects as soon as I can, impatient to restore everybody not greatly in fault themselves to tolerable comfort, and to have done with all the rest.' Compare Austen's use of this technique with Forster's and think about the way this personalisation of the narrative voice might affect the reader.

▲ Maggie Smith as Charlotte in 1986 film

The relationship between the all-seeing narrator and the reader is significant. Sometimes the reader is addressed in such a way as to 'break the fourth wall' by acknowledging the worlds within and outside the text. An example of this is when Forster suggests that Lucy's behaviour is utterly transparent: 'It is obvious enough for the reader to conclude, "She loves young Emerson"' (p.161). This technique acknowledges the direct line of communication between the narrator and narratee. Forster also uses the first person 'I believe' at one point, which further personalises the authorial voice and brings it closer to the reader.

In the early years of the twentieth century some modernist novelists and critics began to question the use of omniscient narrators and try out more experimental fictional forms such as the so-called 'stream of consciousness', a narrative technique that tries to get inside the mind of a character as opposed to describing them from the outside. This literary device aims to mimic the protagonist's thought processes in a way that is startlingly different to Forster's mainly traditional way of telling his story through the eyes of an all-seeing narrator.

Given the time period in which it was written, *A Room with a View* often seems surprisingly relaxed and informal. The narrative voice comes across as approachable and urbane – even chatty at times. As an example, let's look closely at the opening of Chapter 14:

> Of course Miss Bartlett accepted. And, equally of course, she felt sure that she would prove a nuisance, and begged to be given an inferior spare room – something with no view, anything. Her love to Lucy. And, equally of course, George Emerson could come to tennis on the Sunday week.

(p.148)

Two of the sentences in this short paragraph begin with 'and' and include the repeated phrase 'equally of course' to stress the inevitability of what is happening. The second sentence is an example of a distanced form of indirect speech. In effectively quoting Charlotte's letter accepting the invitation and hinting at Lucy's irritated reaction to it, Forster captures both Charlotte's habitual, tiresomely self-deprecating whingeing and, by implication, Lucy's cross response. The omniscient narrator's observation of Lucy's thoughts about Cecil – 'really she must overhaul herself and settle everything up before she married him' – is another example of the same technique (p.163). What we hear with painful clarity here is Lucy's inner voice, or at least the one she's desperately trying to cling on to, even though her thoughts and feelings are not expressed in direct speech.

Another feature of Forster's narrative voice is his tendency to describe the thoughts and reactions of his characters in deceptively simple but highly incisive sentences. One example of this is the description of Mr Beebe reflecting on Lucy: 'The two main facts were clear. She had behaved splendidly and he had helped her. He could not expect to master the details of so big a change in the girl's life' (p.199). We can infer that Mr Beebe is a logical thinker even when blind to what is happening in front of him.

Forster can also open a paragraph with a short, simple sentence and then develop its central idea through a series of increasingly longer ones. The paragraph which begins 'Miss Bartlett burst into florid gratitude' (p.196) does exactly this, as does the opening paragraph of Chapter 7 which builds its 'general sense of groping and bewilderment' by beginning and ending with simple statements but wanders through relative complexity in the middle. These paragraphs are constructed like a piece of music, beginning and ending quietly, but going through a fast and loud passage in the middle.

Another significant feature of Forster's narrative style is the way in which it seems to take it for granted that the reader is intelligent and well educated enough to understand a very wide framework of cultural and artistic references. The reader is expected to 'get' Mr Beebe's response to Lucy's playing of Beethoven's sonata (p.31) and to share his distaste for the Mozart Lucy 'tinkles' away at after jilting Cecil. Mr Emerson quotes the poets Tennyson and Housman from memory and George is reading the work of the modern novelist Samuel Butler. Art, sculpture and architecture is venerated and the Phaethon/Persephone joke about the Italian cab driver and his girlfriend only works if you know who these characters were in Greek mythology. Again, Forster seems to assume that the reader will notice and smile as Cecil confuses the Renaissance artists Michelangelo and Leonardo.

But times change. While all this suggests that Forster was trying to set up a close relationship with his original 1908 readership, the social, cultural and historical context in which *A Room with a View* was originally produced and the twenty-first-century world we live in today mean that we might now interpret the novel as aimed at a very narrow cross-section of the reading public. Indeed a left-wing thinker – like Mr Emerson – might very well draw attention to the way in which fetishising certain types of learning and setting them up as somehow superior to others is another way of seizing power and control.

To counteract the charge of elitism or cultural snobbery, it's worth looking at how Forster pokes fun at Mr Beebe for never having heard of A.E. Housman and Samuel Butler because they are contemporary writers who wouldn't have featured in Mr Beebe's (or Cecil's or Mr Eager's) very traditional classical education (p.130). Perhaps this suggests that as a liberal thinker himself, Forster wants people to be more open-minded about literature, art and culture than many of his narrowly educated contemporaries were (and perhaps still are today). Ironically, of course, the public school/Oxbridge educational pathway that has left Mr Beebe so adrift from modern culture is the very one Forster himself followed. It seems clear that he saw many shortcomings in the narrowly defined fields of learning that were then still very much dominant.

CRITICAL VIEW

Cambridge scholar and critic, F.R. Leavis (1895–1978), advocated an approach to studying literature that emphasised the importance of analysing a text in depth for itself, ignoring contextual factors, which he dismissed as 'extra-critical pryings and impartings'. Leavis criticised *A Room with a View* for its 'curious spinsterish inadequacy in the immediate presentation of love'. Read the rest of Leavis' 1938 essay online at www.unz.org/Pub/Scrutiny-1938sep-00185 and see how far you agree or disagree with his view of the novel.

Sociologist Pierre Bourdieu came up with the term 'cultural capital' to mean everything you have that isn't money that allows or prevents you from moving up or down the ladder of social class. This includes your educational level and the leisure pursuits you choose – and, of course, the books you read. If you think about cultural capital as your personal stake in society and how far you fit in, is it possible that some readers will be alienated by Forster's range of elite cultural references?

Language

The novel's title

E.M. Forster signals the central themes of the novel with a deceptively simple yet powerfully evocative title which gets straight to the heart of things. The room in the Pension Bertolini offers a perfect view in a literal sense: a picture-postcard vision of historic Florence and the River Arno. The offering of the room by the Emersons and the acceptance of it by Lucy and Charlotte forge a link between these two sets of strangers that underpins the whole text. On another level, of course, the view that meets Lucy's eyes is metaphorical; it connotes a vision of the new world as it was beginning to unfold in the first decade of the twentieth century. (The significance of 'rooms' and 'views' is discussed in detail on page 66 of this study guide.)

Names and naming

The names in *A Room with a View* are significant. The surname 'Honeychurch' suggests two traditional, perhaps shallow, symbols of the middle class. They favour sweet things (and ignore what they dislike) and regard churchgoing as a respectable way of life. The surname 'Vyse', on the other hand, sounds like 'vice' which connotes the entrapment Lucy would have suffered had she married Cecil. Ralph Waldo Emerson (1803–82) was a famous American poet and philosopher whom Forster may want us to connect with Mr Emerson and George. Ralph Waldo Emerson once declared that 'To be yourself in a world that is constantly trying to make you something else is the greatest accomplishment', and this is precisely the sort of thing Forster's bravely free-thinking Mr Emerson might have said. Then again, Forster has deliberately given Miss Lavish and Mr Eager, even the Vyses, names which describe their rather stereotyped stock characters or characteristics. In this he is following a long literary tradition; the drunkard Sir Toby Belch in Shakespeare's *Twelfth Night* is another example of this technique. In using this consciously archaic and ironic signposting technique, Forster creates a further level of comic irony that distances the reader from these minor characters.

Irony and humour

Irony in literature can take several forms:

- **Verbal irony** occurs when words are used to imply something different from their surface meaning.
- **Situational irony** is the gap between what is expected to happen and what actually takes place.
- **Dramatic irony** is what happens when the reader or audience is more aware of what's going on than the character or characters themselves.

A good example of Forster employing verbal irony, i.e. using an amusingly sarcastic phrase to imply the opposite of what it appears to mean, is his comment in Chapter 1 that Lucy had 'not yet acquired decency'. What he really means the reader to infer is that Lucy is in fact far more courteous and naturally polite than anyone else present and that she is showing this by rising to her feet and greeting Mr Beebe with open enthusiasm rather than being suppressed by a cold and distant code of 'decency'. It's an effective way of expressing an idea very succinctly without labouring it and is crucial to Forster's style.

In terms of situational irony, or the disconnection between what is expected to happen and what actually occurs, the whole text can be seen to exemplify this; the plot has Lucy refusing to marry Cecil as expected, because of the feelings she has for George.

Dramatic irony can also be seen throughout the novel, as the reader knows that Lucy and George are compatible long before Lucy finally becomes aware of it.

Forster's humour often consists in lightness of touch and in his ironic observation of his characters. Charlotte and Miss Lavish may be seen as stock comic characters while Cecil *thinks* he's clever and witty, but certainly isn't; he seems insolent when patronising Lucy and sneering at the Emersons. Forster, however, rather like Mr Beebe within the text itself, is a detached observer who watches and comments on the characters. Thus we get his gently mocking summary of the nervous but intrepid Miss Alans, who regard going abroad as 'a species of warfare', as if venturing into the depths of a terrifying jungle miles from civilisation. The ladies' comical obsession with 'clothes, guidebooks, mackintosh squares and digestive bread' encourages the reader to smile at their quaint 'little Englander' attitude (p.200).

On the very first page of the novel Forster mocks the sort of tourists who stay in places like the Pension Bertolini, which is run by a Londoner, much to Lucy's disappointment. These Englishmen and -women abroad are absurdly obsessed with avoiding having anything to do with Italians while in Italy. He repeats the word 'English' four times in a single paragraph to satirise this attitude.

TASK

As you read the novel, list key examples of Forster's use of irony. Work out and make notes on the subtext of each example. What is Forster inferring about the character whose thoughts he is describing or from what they say?

Dialogue

Much of Forster's narrative and characterisation is driven by naturalistic dialogue which usually rattles along with dramatic panache. He keeps it moving by not

Taking it further

Compare Forster's use of dialogue in the paralleled scenes between Lucy and her two lovers in Chapters 17 and 20. Then, if possible, watch one or both of the film adaptations of the text to see how closely the screenwriters have stuck to the original. Where have cuts been made and to what extent are they justifiable? Has anything essential been lost?

using explanatory third person words ('he said', etc.) when only two people are speaking as in the long scene between Lucy and Cecil in Chapter 17 or the intimate lovers' banter between Lucy and George in Chapter 20. He also allows characters to reveal themselves through the way they speak, with their speech styles very much linked to their personalities, beliefs and ideas. The dialogue given to the frank, open and transparently honest Mr Emerson perfectly encapsulates his character and is, of course, the reason why he causes such consternation among the other English tourists in Florence. Moreover Forster often allows his more obnoxious characters to damn themselves through what they say. Tiresome Charlotte Bartlett is one such; the writer hardly ever describes her or comments on her behaviour, instead presenting her almost wholly through her dialogue.

Images, motifs and symbols

Writers often use related language patterns and clusters to infuse certain characters with particular associations, evoke a specific mood or atmosphere, or draw attention to a particularly significant theme. In *A Room with a View* Forster uses recurring images, motifs and symbols to create a sense of dramatic and structural coherence and you should think about the ways in which the overarching effects of his images, motifs and symbols enrich the unique atmosphere of the text.

- ▼ **Violets:** When George first kisses the virginal and innocent Lucy, they are in a field of gorgeous spring violets 'irrigating the hillside with blue' (p.70). Some critics have interpreted that moment at Fiesole as Lucy's symbolic loss of virginity. From that moment she is no longer innocent in the sense that she now has new feelings of physical longing for George which she tries and fails to suppress. She is also later fearful that if Cecil finds out it will make a difference because he wants her 'untouched'. The moment can also be read, of course, as a mere opportunistic kiss that changes Lucy's view of her position and power. In traditional Christian art – in paintings of the Nativity for example – violets symbolise both Mary's chastity and the Christ Child's meekness. Their presence in the scene can be interpreted as connoting Lucy's loss of innocence at that moment. Significantly it is the violets which Lucy instantly recognises as an account of her own experience when she reads a version of it in Eleanor Lavish's romance novel (see below). So does George who, aroused by the memory, kisses her for the second time a few lines after hearing it read aloud.

- ▼ **Water:** Another traditional recurring symbol in *A Room with a View* is water. It's a view of the River Arno which Lucy wants and beside which she walks back to the pension with George in Chapter 4. The flooded puddle in which Freddy likes to bathe is nicknamed 'The Sacred Lake' and it's the ritually cleansing water of the Christian font which Mr Emerson has rejected for George. Most religions, thought systems and cultures associate water with three things – purity, fertility and the source of life – which can all be seen as tying in with Forster's purpose. When George, Freddy and Mr Beebe splash about in The Sacred Lake their childlike behaviour in the idyllic natural setting suggests purity, liberty and innocence. At the beginning of the novel Lucy is pure. Her eventual relationship with George will presumably bring children and their fresh relationship based on feelings and truth rather than on convention represents a form of new life.

◥ **Books:** Forster gives symbolic value to books and reading throughout the novel.

    ◥ **The Emersons' books** are an impressive and eclectic mix of established and contemporary texts. Forster wants us to see that they are eager and free-thinking intellectuals – much more so than, for example, Mr Beebe. On their reading list is Lord Byron (1788–1824), a best-selling Romantic poet who was a social, cultural and political radical. Samuel Butler's novel The Way of All Flesh first appeared in 1903. Edward Gibbon (1737–94) was a rational Enlightenment historian whose The History of the Decline and Fall of the Roman Empire appeared from 1776–89 in several volumes. Schopenhauer (1788–1860) and Nietzsche (1844–1900) were German philosophers who symbolise the forward-looking, free-thinking attitude of both father and son in comparison with Cecil and Mrs Honeychurch who are looking conservatively back to Victorian times.

    ◥ **Lucy's Baedeker** is a symbol of her adherence to the conventions of her class – but then Miss Lavish confiscates it.

    ◥ **Miss Lavish's trashy novel**, full of 'Love, murder, abduction, revenge', tells us a lot about her. The fact that the heroine's name is to be 'Leonora', a near-anagram of her own name, Eleanor, is an ironic comment on her self-absorption. The fact that she is prepared to use George and Lucy's kiss to boost her sales figures shows the truth of her smug admission that 'We literary hacks are shameless creatures. I believe there's no secret of the human heart into which we wouldn't pry.'

◥ Lucy's music:

    ◥ **Beethoven's sonatas:** Music is sometimes the only way in which Lucy can express her turbulent emotions and she uses Beethoven's sonatas as a kind

> ### Build critical skills
>
> Analyse Forster's narrative methods in the passage from Chapter 15 which runs from '"It isn't worth reading"' to 'He turned over the leaves' (p.179). This is where Cecil unwittingly reads aloud Miss Lavish's description of the kiss between 'Leonora' and 'Antonio' in front of Lucy and George, while the horrified Lucy thinks that 'she has gone mad'.

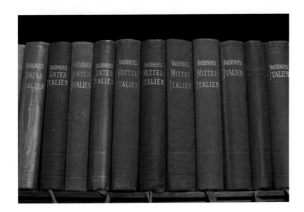

◀ Early twentieth-century Baedeker guides to Italy

65

ingénue: a
stock innocent
young maiden in
literature.

of psychological safety valve that means she can maintain the role of perfect and innocent **ingénue** the rest of time. As a pianist, Lucy is 'no longer either deferential or patronising; no longer either rebel or a slave' (Chapter 3). Instead, she can be herself, unfettered by the dictates of her class and gender. As she matures, however, music becomes simply 'the employment of a child' – a hobby or pastime – and no longer an adequate substitute for real life. The time to 'play' is over as the time to live approaches.

▼ **Miss Lucy Ashton's song:** Lucy Ashton is the doomed heroine of Sir Walter Scott's tragic novel *The Bride of Lammermoor* (1819), a text that inspired the Italian composer Gaetano Donizetti's hugely successful 1835 opera version *Lucia di Lammermoor*. The tragedy of the fragile Lucy/Lucia, whose life is ruined by a bitter family feud, is a stark warning against betraying one's heart for material security. Clearly Lucy Honeychurch isn't giving her all as Donizetti's Lucia in the opera's famously challenging 'mad scene', although Forster doesn't tell us exactly whose musical setting she is singing. It may well be the version by Henry Bishop (1786–1855) who wrote *Home Sweet Home* and many other popular and commercially successful ballads.

▼ **Indoors and outdoors; rooms and views:** Open outdoor (often Italian) spaces – views – symbolise freedom of expression and uninhibited joy. When George and Lucy kiss, their feelings are presented as cohering with the organic natural beauty of the Tuscan countryside. In contrast, stuffy indoor (English) spaces – rooms – connote stifling entrapment and oppressive restrictions. Lucy's encounters with Cecil usually take place inside to symbolise the extent to which she is imprisoned by the rigid social codes of her society. As the novel opens, Lucy's disappointment at not being given a room with a view encapsulates her frustration at being prevented from imaginatively exploring the world outside the window; as it ends she has found a way into that wider world with George.

Build critical skills

Analyse Forster's narrative methods in the passage from Chapter 15 which runs from '"How do you like this view of ours, Mr Emerson?"' (p.165) to 'according to her son – had seen as far as Hindhead' (p.166). This is where Lucy and George discuss the summer scenery of the South Downs around them, in the company of Cecil.

Build critical skills

Our final view of Lucy is of her indoors with George, still looking out at the world as opposed to participating in it. How far do you agree that Forster presents her attempt to find a new way of living as only partly successful?

Target your thinking

- What different critical positions might be applied to *A Room with a View* to extend your knowledge of the text? (**AO1**)
- How can understanding *A Room with a View* within a broad range of contexts deepen your understanding of the text and the ways in which different readers might respond to it? (**AO3**)
- What links might be traced between *A Room with a View* and various other literary texts? (**AO4**)
- How can applying various critical approaches enrich your understanding of *A Room with a View* and the ways in which different readers might interpret it? (**AO5**)

Biographical context

Edward Morgan Forster was born in London in 1879, the only child of Alice and Edward Morgan Forster Senior, an architect who died when his son was very young.

Financially well-off enough not to need to earn his living, Forster in fact worked throughout his life as an author, teacher, critic and essayist. When he arrived at King's College, Cambridge, in 1897, he made friends with several like-minded liberal thinkers and was elected an 'Apostle', a member of an elite intellectual discussion group. Several of its members – including the economist John Maynard Keynes, the essayist and critic Lytton Strachey and the publisher Leonard Woolf – later became affiliated with the so-called Bloomsbury set. (There is more information on the Bloomsbury set in the 'Literary Contexts' section on pages 71–3 of this study guide.)

During a year spent travelling in Italy and Greece, Forster collected much of the material for *A Room with a View*, in the autumn of 1901; for example, he and his mother Alice stayed at the Pensione Simi in Florence, which became the model for the Pension Bertolini. His Italian travels had already inspired two other novels by the time *A Room with a View* was published in 1908: *Where Angels Fear to Tread* (1905) and *The Longest Journey* (1907).

▲ E.M. Forster

> **Context**
>
> The Bloomsbury Group was an influential early-twentieth-century collective of thinkers, writers and artists who lived in or near the Bloomsbury area of London. Modern and liberal in their outlook, the group's cultural impact was vast in such diverse fields as literature, philosophy and economics.

Taking it further ▶

Find out more about Forster's life, using online sources or some of the books listed at the end of this guide. Think carefully about the possible impact upon his work of the other Bloomsbury Group writers and thinkers he knew to develop your understanding of where Forster fits into English literary history.

Like his fellow Bloomsbury Group colleagues Virginia Woolf, John Maynard Keynes and Lytton Strachey, Forster was homosexual. Because homosexuality was illegal at the time it is never mentioned overtly in the writings he published in his lifetime, although he did refer to it in private letters. Forster's novel *Maurice*, about a homosexual relationship, was written in 1910–13 and circulated to friends but not published until 1972, after the author's death in 1970.

Forster's most famous and highly acclaimed – and last – novel is *A Passage to India*, published in 1924 with a lot of encouragement from his close friends Leonard and Virginia Woolf. After the publication of this last great work of fiction, Forster continued to write short stories, articles and reviews as well as teaching and working for the Red Cross in Egypt during World War I. *Aspects of the Novel*, a work of literary criticism based on a series of lectures he gave at Trinity College, Cambridge, was published in 1927 to considerable praise. Following the death of his mother in 1945 Forster was offered an honorary fellowship at King's College, Cambridge, where he had studied as an undergraduate, and he spent the rest of his life there. During the second half of his long life he continued to write essays and reviews. He refused a knighthood in 1949, but became a member of the exclusive and extremely prestigious Order of Merit (OM) just a year before his death in June 1970 at the age of 91.

Political, social and historical contexts

A changing political landscape: The rise of socialism and the road to war

A Room with a View is set at exactly the time it was written. In 1908 the Liberal government led by Herbert Asquith was beginning to challenge the status quo; within a couple of years Asquith's radical Chancellor of the Exchequer, the Welsh firebrand David Lloyd George, was planning his famous People's Budget, which had the clearly stated aim of taxing the rich to pay for social welfare programmes for the poor. In April 1909, Lloyd George declared that:

> *This is a war Budget. It is for raising money to wage implacable warfare against poverty and squalidness. I cannot help hoping and believing that before this generation has passed away, we shall have advanced a great step towards that good time, when poverty, and the wretchedness and human degradation which always follows in its camp, will be as remote to the people of this country as the wolves which once infested its forests.*

(www.nationalarchives.gov.uk/
education/britain1906to1918/g2/
gallery2.htm)

TASK

Create a visual representation of the contextual background to *A Room with a View*. This might be a timeline or wall display that illustrates the key historical, political, social and cultural contexts to which E.M. Forster was responding.

The seismic political struggle between the Liberal government that controlled the House of Commons and the mainly Conservative peers who dominated the House of Lords raged for three years. The Conservatives saw the attempt to tax their property as an all-out attack based on class war and bitterly resisted the Liberals' attempts to get their finance bill through the House of Lords.

King Edward VII died during the budget crisis and in the end it was his son, George V, who was persuaded to agree to the creation of several hundred new Liberal peers to cancel out the inbuilt Conservative majority in the Lords. To avoid this nuclear option, the Conservative peers allowed the finance bill to pass. From that time on, traditionally the Lords has never tried to overrule a finance bill that has already been passed by the Commons.

A Room with a View's Mr Emerson is a socialist, as Mr Beebe acknowledges to the horrified Charlotte in Chapter 1. Socialists argue that money, land and property should be owned and controlled, perhaps communally, by the working people who generate it rather than by land or factory owners who control the workers and pass the resultant wealth from one generation to another within their own families. The Scottish miner Keir Hardie became the first elected socialist (Labour) MP in 1892. Eminent people such as the playwright George Bernard Shaw (1856–1950) were also actively and vociferously supporting the cause through the Fabian Society which he co-founded with Beatrice and Sidney Webb and the novelist H.G. Wells in 1884 to promote evolutionary (gradual) socialism. Organisations such as these eventually fed into the modern Labour Party which emerged in its present form in 1900.

Mr Emerson is not presented as an aggressive political activist in the novel. His manner is gentle and reasonable and he never criticises the wealth or lifestyle of the people he speaks to, although he is very forthright. Modern readers of *A Room with a View* need to understand, however, the fear with which many middle- and upper-class Britons regarded anything to do with socialism in the time period in which the novel was written and set. Socialism was seen as a declaration of class war – an all-out assault on the traditional way of life of the well-off, whether their money had come from centuries of land owning ('old wealth') or from successful entrepreneurialism during the expansion of the manufacturing industries at home and in the colonies during the eighteenth and nineteenth centuries ('new money').

Mr Emerson is never rude but as he believes in total equality; he will not defer to – let alone grovel to – people of a supposedly higher social class. He addresses everyone he speaks to as if they were his equals, and this is what Mr Beebe means when he says that Mr Emerson 'has no tact and no manners' (p.9).

International politics was also increasingly volatile during this period. The year 1908 was the midpoint between the accession of Edward VII and the outbreak of the Great War. England's increasingly friendly diplomatic relations with France were causing great disquiet in Germany and increasing tension between the major European powers. The situation was complicated by the strong personal dislike felt for Edward VII by his unstable and jealous nephew Wilhelm, the German Emperor (Kaiser). *A Room with a View*, therefore, takes place against a backdrop of escalating international tension; despite Edward VII's 1908 visit to Germany, the British press was publishing increasingly hostile articles about the arms race that appeared to be underway as the Kaiser built up the German Navy in an aggressive attempt to rival the Royal Navy – then the greatest in the world. Although there had not been a full-scale continental war in Europe since

▲ Timothy Spall as Mr Emerson and Rafe Spall as George Emerson in the 2007 film (father and son playing father and son)

the defeat of Napoleon at Waterloo in 1815, the days of peace were in fact numbered and the terrible conflict which engulfed millions of young men like Cecil, George and Freddy was looming on the horizon.

The rise of the suffragettes

In June 1908, the year *A Room with a View* was published, there was a suffragette rally in Hyde Park attended by approximately 300,000 people. Forster's presentation of Lucy's development as an independent thinker and, eventually, wife, is therefore highly topical.

'Feminism' is a late-twentieth-century term. In Forster's time most people would have said that the focus of the campaigning by the Women's Social and Political Union (WSPU) founded in 1903 by Emmeline Pankhurst and her daughters Christabel and Sylvia was to get women the vote. The WSPU were known as the Suffragettes. There was another, more peaceful, campaigning group: the Suffragists. Largely because they had had to take over men's jobs during World War I, women over 30 were eventually granted the right to vote in 1918, with equal voting rights for all adults over the age of 21 coming into force in 1928. Within the novel, Mrs Honeychurch refers disapprovingly to the WSPU's activities. There were demonstrations from 1906 and direct activities such as arson and vandalism, with many women being sent to prison where some were subjected to force-feeding to confound their hunger strikes.

Context

Following a public outcry to the force-feeding of hunger-striking suffragettes in prison, the Liberal government passed the notorious Prisoners (Temporary Discharge for Ill Health) Act of 1913, also known as the Cat and Mouse Act. The Act meant that women would be released from prison when they became extremely ill, only to be sent back when they recovered their health. The nickname given to this oppressive piece of legislation refers to the way a cat plays with a mouse to prolong its torment before killing it.

▲ 1913 Poster protesting against the Cat and Mouse Act

Equality means more than the right to vote, though, and women have gone on campaigning through to the present day for the same job opportunities as men. This brings with it issues such as child care and maternity leave. In Forster's time it was almost unthinkable for a middle- or upper-class married woman to work outside the home. It was common for the employment of female teachers, civil servants and other professionals to be terminated when they married – the so-called 'marriage bar' – right up until World War I. Yet there were some small but significant signs of change. In 1908, Edith Morley, suffragette and Fabian, was appointed to the post of Professor of English at University College Reading, the first woman to hold an academic 'chair' in a British university. In the same year the medical pioneer Dr Elizabeth Garrett Anderson became the first woman to become an elected mayor.

Literary and cultural contexts

The Bloomsbury Group

By the time he was writing *A Room with a View,* Forster was associating with and influenced by a set of people who came to be known as the Bloomsbury Group. These were men and women, mostly libertarian rebels of various sorts, who met informally in the London (Bloomsbury) flat of the Stephen sisters. Still both unmarried, they were to become novelist Virginia Woolf and artist Vanessa Bell. Also in the group were the influential economist John Maynard Keynes, subversive biographer Lytton Strachey and writer/publisher David 'Bunny' Garnett among others. Forster was particularly friendly with Leonard Woolf, who became Virginia Woolf's husband. Many of the group were gay or bisexual and all were trying to break free of societal restraints. Forster's Lucy Honeychurch would have been intrigued. Her cousin Charlotte Bartlett would have been, outwardly at least, horrified and probably subliminally jealous of the group's free-thinking.

Modernism

Modernism is a massive umbrella term linking many different trends, developments, experiments and changes mainly in literature, art and music between – roughly – the last quarter of the nineteenth century and the outbreak of World War II in 1939. From the 1950s onward a newer still set of trends are lumped together as 'postmodernism'.

Modernism usually involved experimenting with form rather than presenting a work of art – whatever its form – in the conventional time-honoured way. 'Modernists' in art include people such as Pablo Picasso who painted *Les Demoiselles d'Avignon* (1907), a large oil painting of a group of naked prostitutes from a Barcelona brothel. A riot of colour and shape that makes no attempt to be naturalistic or representational, this painting upset many people (including several fellow painters) because it was so different from what had gone before. The ultra-conservative English visitors to Florence in *A Room with a View* are, apparently, oblivious of these developments in the world of art and keen only to admire the work of painters such as Giotto from many centuries earlier.

In music Arnold Schoenberg (1874–1951) was experimenting with the 12-tone scale which meant using every available note at will rather than using the conventional tradition of working mostly with 8 notes in a chosen key. This atonality makes it sound strikingly original even over a century after it was written. One of his string quartets (No. 2 in F sharp), premiered in 1908, the year *A Room with a View* was published, is a very long way from Lucy Honeychurch's Beethoven, Schumann and Mozart.

In literature modernistic experiments with form often involved a move away from omniscient narration, enlarging brief moments into something very significant, intense and drawn out or characterised by an innovative use of language. Writers such as Virginia Woolf (*Mrs Dalloway*, 1925) and James Joyce (*Ulysses*, 1922) came to emphasise the consciousness of their characters rather than what happens to them. There was also a tendency for modernist authors to explore unconventional sexual relationships, as D.H. Lawrence did extensively. Set against these radical innovators, it seems clear why Forster is not grouped with them. Although written during the early years of modernism, *A Room with a View* is a novel still very much within the tradition of realism, in that nothing happens in it that couldn't quite easily occur in real life. It is set out in chapters and told chronologically by an omniscient narrator. Having said this, his central protagonist is a woman with sexual feelings which eventually lead her to a triumphantly unconventional marriage outside her own social class and that is a thoroughly modernist concept. And, although Forster certainly doesn't go as far as, say, his Bloomsbury associate Virginia Woolf's 'stream of consciousness' experiments, he does reflect on his character's interior thought processes in some depth and detail.

TASK

Using the information provided in this section, explore the ways in which *A Room with a View* can be seen as a traditional text and in what ways it can be seen as modernist.

TASK

As you apply different critical positions to *A Room with a View*, keep a detailed reading diary. Discussing your interpretations with other students can also help you to challenge and develop your own ideas.

Critical contexts

Ways of thinking about texts

As an A-level student, you are required to demonstrate an understanding that the meaning of a text is not 'fixed' and that at various places within a text different interpretations are possible. These different interpretations may be supported by reference to the ideas of named critics or particular critical perspectives, but may also emerge from your own discussions with other students and your teacher. Either way, what really matters is that you have come to a personal interpretation of the novel through an understanding of a variety of ways in which its meanings are made.

Critical approaches

In 1967 the French literary theorist Roland Barthes wrote a hugely influential essay called 'The Death of the Author' in which he argued that the idea of an author or authority led people to believe it was possible to decode and hence explain the essential 'meaning' of a text. For Barthes, the multiple different ways of making meaning in language and the fact that it is impossible to know the author's state of mind pretty much made a mockery of the idea of a 'knowable text'. The Marxist Barthes saw the concept of the author as another method of transforming a text into a consumer product which could be used up and replaced in a bourgeois westernised capitalist culture.

While the 'death of the author' theory might at first seem to suggest Roland Barthes effectively cut the reader's safety rope and left him or her dangling off a literary cliff, in fact his ideas can be seen as heralding the 'birth of the reader' and so empowering him or her. The reader-response approach to literature suggests that writers and readers *collaborate* to make meanings and that our responses will depend upon our own experiences, ideas and values. Unlike literary theories or critical positions which concentrate on the author, content or form of the text, reader-response theory privileges the role of the active reader in creating textual meanings. If you remember this, you may well feel more confident in assessing the performances, interpretations and literary-critical points of view you encounter. Moreover, by setting the novel at the centre of an intertextual web of contexts and connections, you can start to trace the assumptions underlying both *A Room with a View* itself and the responses of various readers to the text. By resisting the notion of fixed meanings, you are free to make the most of the shifting and unstable nature of the text itself. Thus while this section covers a variety of modern critical approaches that can shed considerable light on the novel, remember that you too are a critic, and as such you should always try to form your own interpretation of the text.

Feminist criticism

Feminist critics are interested in how women are represented in literature, challenging dominant traditional attitudes and ideas about how female characters (who are often seen through the eyes of male writers) feel, act and think. Feminist criticism challenges patriarchal assumptions by unpacking the gender stereotyping embodied in a text and exploring how such stereotypes can be undermined and resisted and has developed over the last 50 years or so as a way of studying literature with these issues in mind.

Given that *A Room with a View* was written in 1908, Lucy Honeychurch may be viewed as a progressive and forward-looking character in that she eventually assertively rejects her mother's values and seizes a relationship which will grant her 'equality beside the man she loved' (p.115). Feminist critics might note how Lucy begins to assert her independence in rebellion against the repressive Victorian attitudes exemplified by Charlotte, going into the city alone to buy postcards and witnessing a distressingly violent event. Yet a feminist critical perspective might still interpret Lucy's decision to marry at all as following the traditional patriarchal convention; had Forster been really brave he could have sent her off to Italy as George's lover or mistress. Then again, that would probably have seen the novel criticised or even banned for obscenity.

Build critical skills

As well as Roland Barthes, other critics closely associated with reader-response theory include the German Wolfgang Iser (1926–2007) and the American Stanley Fish (b. 1938). You might wish to research their ideas online to see how far you think they may be applied to *A Room with a View*.

TASK

As you read the novel, list all the occasions when Forster presents Lucy rebelling against the constraints of her social class and the customs of her day.

It is unarguable that the character of Lucy drives the narrative. She plays the major role in the text, while core issues associated with traditional male and female gender roles such as marriage, homemaking, education, work and civil rights are extensively debated within the context of the novel. Relationships between female characters are varied, vividly drawn, interestingly problematic and highly convincing and male–female relationships are analysed and dissected in forensic detail.

Build critical skills

In his essay 'Forster's Trespasses: Tourism and Cultural Politics,' James Buzard describes Lucy as 'a powerless and sexually naïve protagonist' who 'lurks behind the screen of custom, class and sex' (*E.M. Forster*, 1995). How far would a feminist critic agree that Lucy is powerless in view of what happens later in the novel? Is there another way of interpreting her caution?

Build critical skills

A Historicist view of *A Room with a View* might stress that the 'triumph' of George Emerson over Cecil Vyse in the competition for Lucy Honeychurch's hand in marriage reveals the rise of the middle class and the decline of the aristocracy in the early years of the twentieth century. How do you respond to this view of the text?

CRITICAL VIEW

In her influential work *The Laugh of the Medusa* (1975), the French feminist critic Hélène Cixous (b. 1937) coins the terms '*écriture féminine*' and 'white ink' to articulate what she saw as the challenges women face to find a way of expressing female difference in texts. Her standpoint is that language is not neutral, but forces women writers to communicate in a 'male' voice, encapsulating patriarchal oppression, which does not allow them to truly express themselves; *écriture féminine* theoretically offers a way for women writers to escape this trap. To what extent, in your view, is E.M. Forster, successful in creating the central character of Lucy Honeychurch?

Political criticism

The German philosopher and political thinker Karl Marx (1818–83) was the founder of modern communism. In *The Communist Manifesto* (1848) Marx stated, 'The history of all hitherto existing society is the history of class struggles.' Thus a Marxist literary critical perspective sees works of literature as inevitably conditioned by and reflective of the economic and political forces of their social context. Political criticism, which might include Historicist and Marxist approaches, reminds us that literary texts are products of a particular set of socio-political circumstances from which they cannot be divorced, and that they are informed by a range of cultural preoccupations and anxieties that manifest themselves regardless of whether they are consciously intended by the writer or not. Historicists remind us how texts engage with the warp and weft of history and look at the ways in which readers often find in texts ideas that confirm their own. Marxist critics see literary texts as material products which are part of – and help to explain – the processes of history, as Terry Eagleton notes:

Marxist criticism is not merely a 'sociology of literature', concerned with how novels get published and whether they mention the working class. Its aim is to explain the literary work more fully; and this means a sensitive attention to its forms, styles and meanings. But it also means grasping those forms, styles and meanings as the product of a particular history.

(Eagleton, *Marxism and Literary Criticism*, 1976)

Marxist critics see capitalism as a system in which most people work to produce goods and services but do not share equally in the benefits of their labour because the ruling class owns the means of production. Hence Marxist critics see literature as inevitably bound up with the economic and political forces of the times in which they were written. The novel's central female character, Lucy, lacks any official social, political and economic authority as a young woman living in the first decades of the twentieth century.

Yet in some ways the narrative constantly exposes and condemns the **stultifying** conservative norms, ideas and values of Edwardian England, together with its laws, religion and system of education. Financially well-off enough to be able to live very comfortably without having to work for a living, Forster felt uneasy about this situation. This may be seen in his presentation of Mr Emerson and George's professional careers in journalism and engineering, and likeable Freddy Honeychurch as a trainee doctor. In contrast Cecil Vyse's proud boast to Mr Beebe that he has no profession – that is, he is a 'gentleman' who does not need to work for a living – is presented as both vulgar and crass (p.94). Zadie Smith has noted how interestingly Forster deals with characters who are 'privately incomed in a world where most people work' and links this to his own experience of 'independent financial security, because it made him feel that he could not understand the experience of the great majority of his fellow men' (Smith, 2003). Aspects of the text that would be well worth reviewing through this critical lens are referenced elsewhere in this study guide, particularly in the 'Chapter summaries and commentaries' and 'Themes' sections, but here is a reminder of those which are particularly worth revisiting:

- The class consciousness that causes Mr Emerson to be snubbed, shunned and sidelined within the context of a strictly hierarchical social structure.
- The division of the labour force, in that Mr Emerson and George work for their livings, whereas Cecil lives off unearned income.
- The presentation of Lennie, the 'gardener's boy'.
- The presentation of the Italian cab driver.

Psychoanalytic criticism

Sigmund Freud published one of the founding texts of psychoanalysis, *The Interpretation of Dreams* (*Die Traumdeutung*), in 1900. Psychoanalytic critics see literature as dreamlike, since both fictions and dreams are inventions

> ### Build critical skills
>
> A Marxist reading of *A Room with a View* might suggest that human relationships are inevitably warped and distorted by the forces of a capitalist social and political system and that Lucy is in effect just another a commodity to be bought and traded. How do you respond to this view of the text?

stultifying: suffocating and inhibiting.

of the mind that, although based on reality, are obviously not literally true. Psychoanalytic critics look at the significance of the subconscious in order to explore literary representation of character; working with the theories developed by Freud over a century ago they analyse the effect of dreams, fantasies, unconscious desires and aspects of human sexuality, attaching great significance to the underlying hidden meanings of words and actions as revelations of the essential truth about someone's state of mind. Perhaps because it was written at a time when the ideas of Freud were becoming quite widely known in intellectual circles, several key scenes and events within *A Room with a View* lend themselves particularly well to being viewed through this critical lens. Indeed Forster explicitly refers to Freudian psychology at times, inviting his readers to look at the underlying motivations that may be seen to influence the conscious actions of his characters.

One example of how a psychoanalytic reading can be applied to the text is the incident in Chapter 1 when Charlotte Bartlett refuses Mr Emerson's offer to exchange rooms at the pension because she worries that there's an immoral intimacy in moving into a room just vacated by a man. The reader can interpret her behaviour as revealing more about her own repressed sexuality and secret inner longings than any real concern for Lucy's moral welfare. On the other hand right at the end of the novel, George Emerson suggests that 'far down in her heart' – i.e. unconsciously, and in complete negation of all her previous attempts to separate them – Charlotte wanted him and Lucy to be together, and therefore engineered the meeting between Lucy and his father at the rectory. This analysis of Charlotte's motivation, which seems to be endorsed by Forster, can certainly be read as being influenced by Freud.

Of course by far the most important character to look at through this critical lens is Lucy Honeychurch herself. The following examples are some of the ways in which it is possible to examine Lucy's behaviour from this perspective, but you will almost certainly be able to spot others:

- In Chapter 7, just after George has kissed her, Lucy's denial of her true feelings for him can be viewed as displacement illusions predicated upon her burgeoning feelings of mature sexuality being too frightening to be looked at directly. She comes close to admitting to Charlotte that she enjoyed George's kiss and was in fact anticipating and wanting it; 'I am a little to blame. I had silly thoughts. The sky, you know, was gold, and the ground all blue, and for a moment he looked like someone in a book … Heroes – gods – the nonsense of schoolgirls.' Significantly, as she speaks, 'Lucy's body was shaken by deep sighs which nothing could repress'. She also tries to excuse George, telling Charlotte, 'I think he was taken by surprise, just as I was before', as if trying to rationalise away the kiss in rather primitively Freudian psychological terms, dismissing George's action and her own response as impulses driven by their unconscious minds. Doing this means Lucy can avoid confronting head-on the fact that they are both passionate individuals who feel a strong sexual desire for each other. Ironically, of course, the reader can use the same psychological critical perspective to observe that Lucy is telling Charlotte a version of the story that reflects a more socially correct and less dangerous truth.

▼ When staying at Mrs Vyse's London flat in Chapter 11, Lucy has a nightmare that causes her to cry out in her sleep. Mrs Vyse finds her 'sitting upright [in bed] with her hand on her cheek'. This is shortly after Lucy has received a letter from Charlotte urging her to tell her mother about her 'secret' – that is, George's kiss. A nightmare is usually interpreted as the unconscious mind working through a powerful negative emotional response that breaks through to wake the sleeper and leave them feeling panicky and disorientated, and in a state of extreme shock, distress or fear. In *The Interpretation of Dreams* Freud theorised that nightmares suggest the sufferer is reliving a past stressful event. In Freudian terms, Lucy's dream is very clearly an expression of the stressful situation in which she finds herself: a guest in her fiancé's home unable to forget her feelings for another man.

▼ In Chapter 14, Forster uses the language of psychology in a notably direct manner that actually invites the reader to apply such a reading. The narrator describes Lucy using the language of psychology – ironically enough as explained to her by Cecil – to rationalise away her own unconscious desire for George and to further obscure the truth about the depth of George's love for her. As Forster notes teasingly, however, while the reader might see through Lucy's subterfuges all too clearly, that's the easy bit. We can all do that, he suggests. The trickier question is, would the reader see things quite so clearly *if he or she were in Lucy's position themselves*? Of course not:

> Top ten quotation

Lucy faced the situation bravely, though, like most of us, she only faced the situation that encompassed her. She never gazed inwards. If at times strange images rose from the depths, she put them down to nerves. When Cecil brought the Emersons to Summer Street, it had upset her nerves. Charlotte would burnish up past foolishness, and this might upset her nerves. She was nervous at night. When she talked to George – they met again almost immediately at the Rectory – his voice moved her deeply, and she wished to remain near him. How dreadful if she really wished to remain near him! Of course, the wish was due to nerves, which love to play such perverse tricks upon us.

Once she had suffered from 'things that came out of nothing and meant she didn't know what. Now Cecil had explained psychology to her one wet afternoon, and all the troubles of youth in an unknown world could be dismissed.'

It is obvious enough for the reader to conclude, 'She loves young Emerson.' A reader in Lucy's place would not find it obvious. Life is easy to chronicle, but bewildering to practise, and we welcome 'nerves' or any other shibboleth that will cloak our personal desire.

'She loved Cecil; George made her nervous; will the reader explain to her that the phrases should have been reversed?

But the external situation – she will face that bravely.'

(p.161)

Queer theory

The term 'queer theory' was only coined in 1990, but since the late 1960s, as Julie Rivkin and Michael Ryan note, critics had begun to examine the 'history of the oppression of gays, lesbians, and practitioners of sexualities other than those deemed normal by the dominant heterosexual group', as well as the 'countercultures of gay and lesbian writing that existed in parallel fashion with the dominant heterosexual culture' (Rivkin and Ryan, *Literary Theory*, 1999: 888). Queer theory is grounded in a debate about whether a person's sexuality is part of their essential self or socially constructed, questioning the default representation of heterosexuality as 'normal' and exploring 'non-heteronormative' sexual behaviour.

It isn't difficult to find undertones of suppressed homosexuality in *A Room with a View* if you bear in mind E.M. Forster's own sexual orientation. The character of Cecil Vyse is especially worth considering in this context. Mr Beebe seems to recognise something unusual about Cecil which makes him unlikely to be a suitable husband for Lucy. 'Mr Vyse is an ideal bachelor … he's like me – better detached', Beebe notes (p.88). Lucy herself seems to instinctively sense a quality missing in Cecil which she has found, and been deeply disturbed by, in George. Cecil is – clearly – fond of Lucy, regards marriage as a conventional social obligation and is upset when she finally rejects him. The reader senses, however, that Mr Beebe – another man who doesn't seem to be interested in women – is right in that Cecil is not at heart the marrying sort.

An alternative interpretation would be that Mr Beebe has simply observed and identified with Cecil's self-absorption and knows that it is unlikely to make him a happy husband. There is a further hint when Cecil tries to kiss Lucy but 'as he approached … found time to wish that he could recoil' as if he isn't physically drawn to her at all. While it could be that Cecil has no sexual experience, isn't used to kissing and is too nervous to do it with conviction and feeling, this essential innocence, typical of his social class and context, does little to inhibit George and Lucy. As Zadie Smith has noted, Forster's novels contain a group of:

'voyeurs' or 'conscientious abstainer[s]' from life … A specific philosophic type is meant here: this is the man whose life-reading skills are as good as we might hope them to be, but who chooses only to read, to observe, but not to be involved. They are the novel's flaneurs. They invariably think of themselves as 'students of human nature', and they

are condemned by both authors as Aristotle properly condemns them,
as people inured to the responsibilities of proper human involvement.

(Smith, 2003)

Smith includes both Mr Beebe and Cecil Vyse within this group, arguing that 'Forster's voyeurs are very much more layered, and are offered a great deal more empathy' than comparable characters in the novels of Jane Austen:

The most obvious reason is Forster's own personal interest in them.
Several critics have pointed to a sublimated homosexuality here;
they are, to a man, unmarried and uninterested, and as such they are
estranged from the romantic fictions they inhabit.

(Smith, 2003)

George Emerson, who attracts Lucy so much – against the conditioned judgement of some members of her family – is an outsider. Forster was himself a different sort of outsider. He was gay, at a time when homosexuality was illegal. Modern readers and post-modernist critics of *A Room with a View* inevitably see parallels between the cautious, sometimes troubled Forster who often couldn't have what he wanted and George who sees the love of his life clearly before him but thinks it will elude him. 'He is not that sort [that is, homosexual] – no one whom I like seems to be', Forster wrote in 1908 of a man he was attracted to. At the same time we might detect echoes of Forster's own struggles with sexuality in a novel which presents the burgeoning sexuality of a young woman. As critic Claude Summers has observed, it is remarkable that Forster's wrestling with homosexual desire should give rise to one of the richest depictions of heterosexual love in the English language (1983).

TASK

Watch the final scene of each film version two or three times and compare each closely with the printed text. At this point in the story, how do you interpret each director's vision?

Performance context

When studying *A Room with a View*, watching either (or preferably both) the 1985 and 2007 film versions of the text will certainly enhance your ability to engage with the novel as long as you keep asking yourself what has been gained and what has been lost in the move from page to screen.

Assessment Objectives and skills

> **AO1** Articulate informed, personal and creative responses to literary texts using associated concepts and terminology and coherent, accurate written expression

To do well with AO1 you need to write fluently, structuring your essay carefully, guiding your reader through your line of argument and using the sophisticated vocabulary – including critical terminology – that is appropriate to an A-level essay while also remaining clear and cohesive. You will need to use frequent embedded quotations to show detailed knowledge and to demonstrate familiarity with the whole text. Your aim is to produce a well-written academic essay employing appropriate discourse markers to create the sense of a well-shaped argument.

> **AO2** Analyse ways in which meanings are shaped in literary texts

Strong students do not work only on a lexical level, but also write well on the generic and structural elements of the novel so it is useful to start by analysing those larger elements of narrative organisation before considering Forster's language. *A Room with a View* has a fairly conventional structure whose implications you need to consider, especially its division into two halves and the sign-posting chapter headings. Then again in order to discuss language in detail you will need to quote from the novel, analyse that quotation and use it to illuminate your argument. Moreover, since you will at times need to make points about larger generic and organisational features of the text that are much too long to make in full, being able to reference effectively is just as important as mastering the art of embedded quotation. Practise writing in analytical sentences, comprising a brief quotation or close reference, a definition of the feature you intend to analyse, an explanation of how this feature has been used and an evaluation of its effectiveness.

> **AO3** Demonstrate understanding of the significance and influence of the contexts in which literary texts are written

To meet AO3 you need to think about how contexts of production, reception, literature, culture, biography, geography, society, history, genre and intertextuality can affect texts. Place the novel at the heart of the web of contextual factors that you feel have had the most impact on it. Examiners want to see a sense of contextual alertness woven seamlessly into the fabric of your essay rather than a clumsy bolted-on website rehash or some recycled class notes. Show that you understand that literary works contain encoded representations of the cultural, moral, religious, racial and political values of the society from which they emerge and that over time attitudes and ideas change until the views they reflect are no longer widely shared.

AO4	Explore connections across literary texts

If your examination board requires you to compare and contrast one or more texts with *A Room with a View* you must try to find specific points of comparison rather than merely generalising. You will find it easier to make connections between texts (of any kind) if you try to balance them as you write. Remember too that connections are not only about finding similarities – differences are just as interesting. Above all, consider how the comparison illuminates each text. Some connections will be thematic, others generic or stylistic.

AO5	Explore literary texts informed by different interpretations

For this AO you should refer to the opinions of critics and remain alert to those aspects of the novel which are open to interpretation. Your job is to measure your own interpretation against those of other readers. The use of modal verb phrases such as 'may be seen as', 'might be interpreted as' or 'could be represented as' indicates your understanding that different readers will interpret a text in different ways at different times. The key word here is plurality. There is no single meaning or one right answer. Relish getting your teeth into the views of published critics to push forward your own argument, but always remember that meanings in texts are shifting and unstable as opposed to fixed and permanent.

Summary

Overall the hallmarks of a successful A-level essay which hits all five AOs include the following:

- A clear introduction that orientates your reader and outlines your main argument.
- A coherent and conceptualised argument which relates to the question the examiners have presented to you.
- Confident movement around the text rather than a relentless chronological trawl through it.
- Apt and effective quotations or references adapted to make sense within the context of your own sentences.

- ▾ A range of effective points about Forster's narrative methods.
- ▾ A strong and personally engaged awareness of how a text can be interpreted by different readers in different ways at different times.
- ▾ A sense that you are prepared to take on a good range of critical and theoretical perspectives.
- ▾ A conclusion that effectively summarises and consolidates your response and relates it back to your essay title.

Building skills 1: Structuring your writing

This 'Building skills' section focuses upon organising your written responses to convey your ideas as clearly and effectively as possible: the 'how' of your writing as opposed to the 'what'. More often than not, if your knowledge and understanding of *A Room with a View* is sound, a disappointing mark or grade will be down to one of two common mistakes: misreading the question or failing to organise your response economically and effectively. In an examination you'll be lucky if you can demonstrate 5 per cent of what you know about *A Room with a View*. Luckily, if it's the right 5 per cent, that's all you need to gain full marks.

Understanding your examination

It's important to prepare for the specific type of response your examination body sets with regard to *A Room with a View*. You may well be studying the novel as an examination set text for the AQA A Specification, which is an open book paper – i.e. you will have a clean copy of the text available to you in the exam – or as part of an NEA unit for another examination board.

Open book

In an open book exam when you have a copy of *A Room with a View* on the desk in front of you, there can be no possible excuse for failing to quote relevantly, accurately and extensively. To gain a high mark, you are expected to focus in detail on specific passages. Remember, too, that you must not refer to any supporting material such as the Introduction Notes contained within the set edition of your text. If an examiner suspects that you have been lifting chunks of unacknowledged material from such a source, your paper will be referred to the examining body for possible plagiarism.

Closed book

In a closed book exam, because the examiners are well aware that you do not have your text in front of you, their expectations will be different. While you are still expected to support your argument with relevant quotations, close textual references are also encouraged and rewarded. Again, since you will have had to memorise quotations, slight inaccuracies will not be severely punished. Rather than a forensically detailed analysis of a specific section of *A Room with a View*, the examiner will expect you to range more broadly across the play to structure your response.

Non-examined assessment (NEA)

You may be writing about *A Room with a View* within a non-examined assessment unit (i.e. coursework) context. This poses a very different set of challenges from an examination in that incorrect quotations and disorientating arguments are liable to cost you much more dearly. Your essay must be wholly and consistently relevant to the title selected; there's no excuse for going off track if you or your teacher mapped out the parameters of your chosen topic in the first place.

Step 1: Planning and beginning: locate the debate

A very common type of exam question invites you to open a debate about the text by using various trigger words and phrases such as **'consider the view that …'**, **'some readers think that …'** or **'how far do you agree with this view?'** When analysing a question of this sort, the one thing you can be sure of is that exam questions never offer a view that makes no sense at all or one so blindingly obvious that all anyone can do is agree with it. There will always be a genuine interpretation at stake. Similarly many NEA Tasks are written to include a stated view to help give some shape to your writing. Logically, therefore, your introduction needs to address the terms of this debate and sketch out the outlines of how you intend to move the argument forward to orientate the reader. Since it's obviously going to be helpful if you actually know this before you start writing, you really do need to plan before you begin to write.

Undertaking a lively debate about some of the ways in which *A Room with a View* has been, and can be, interpreted is the DNA of your essay. Of course any good argument needs to be honest but to begin by writing 'Yes, I totally agree with this obviously true statement' suggests a fundamental misunderstanding of what studying literature is all about. Any stated view in an examination question is designed to open up critical conversations, not close them down.

Plan your answer by listing points for and against the given view. Aim to see a stated opinion as an interesting way of focusing upon a key facet of *A Room with a View*, like the following student.

Student A

This student is writing a comparative essay on *A Room with a View* and *Jane Eyre* as part of an AQA A exam-style A-level response. The question is:

Compare how the authors of two texts you have studied present ideas about love and social class?

Student A begins like this:

In social class terms and given the constraints limiting members of the middle classes in 1908, Cecil Vyse is a suitable match for Lucy whereas George Emerson is not, any more than Charlotte Brontë's eponymous Jane Eyre is for Mr Rochester. The central protagonists in both novels, as I shall show in this essay, ultimately choose to prioritise love over social class.

The choices aren't polarised, however. Liberally-minded Forster stops short of making the 'well educated, well endowed and not deficient physically' Cecil Vyse ridiculous. He is presented as 'self-conscious' and sometimes arrogant but when Lucy finally breaks off the engagement he proves that he is 'an ascetic at heart', genuinely hurt and humbled. Brontë uses the same adjective 'self-conscious' to describe Mr Rochester's apparently sought-after woman, Blanche Ingram – the decoy. Her 'proud grace' contrasts her with Jane, the one he is really interested in. Like Cecil – although she's much less likeable – Blanche would have been a conventionally suitable marriage of the head but not of the heart. Both novels present the triumph of romantic love, in which, as Forster suggests in his critical work Aspects of the Novel, the novelist can make his characters 'be in love, love and nothing but love, provided that he seems to know everything about them'.

Forster's use of an omniscient narrator allows him to present insights into the thoughts, views and attitudes of several of his characters. He shows Cecil Vyse wanting to cleanse Lucy of the 'Honeychurch taint' because although he finds her stylish he regards her 'suburban ways' as socially inferior. Her social class is, he patriarchially decides, not insuperable. Brontë, in contrast, presents every idea from the standpoint of her single, passionate first person narrator who knows she is socially inferior to Mr Rochester, but – radically for 1848 when Jane Eyre was published – regards herself as his equal in other respects.

Examiner's commentary

This student:

- ❚ selects one or two significant points of connection and begins to develop them in detail
- ❚ splices in her quotations neatly to fit with her own syntax
- ❚ contrasts the contrasting narrative standpoints of the texts
- ❚ signals an awareness of different critical perspectives by using Forster's own view to expand her argument – although without going on to analyse it, just implicitly agreeing with it
- ❚ expresses the personal view that in a romantic novel feelings are likely to overcome pragmatic marriage plans, although this needs to be developed, perhaps by referring to the notion of a conventional 'happy ending'
- ❚ alludes briefly to the different contexts in which the novels were published, but might have done better to link these and explicitly contrast the time periods in terms of their differing representations of the AQA A theme of Love through the Ages.

If the rest of this essay reached this level of performance, it is likely this student would be on course to achieve a notional grade B, as, while this is a promising start, there are clear areas which could have been further developed.

Student B

Like Student A, Student B is answering the AQA A A-level-style comparative Task on *A Room with a View* and *Jane Eyre*.

Student B continues like this:

Both *A Room with a View* and *Jane Eyre* end in marriage which is the traditional fairy story ending for a novel. What is not conventional is that Lucy and George are each marrying out of their social class. George and his father, one of the 'ill-bred people whom one does meet abroad' as the narrator ironically describes him at the beginning of the novel, are respectively a retired journalist and a railway employee. Similarly Jane is, at the outset, a penniless governess and Mr Rochester a wealthy landowner, so there is, by the standards of the day, a class barrier in both cases which is ultimately crossed.

On the other hand, because of their status and Mr Emerson's tactlessness, the general view at the Pension Bertolini is that the Emersons don't know their place. For the modern reader this creates a sense of indignation and sympathy for the kindly outspoken underdog, although many readers in 1908 when the novel was written might have felt differently. Sixty years earlier the attitude of Blanch Ingram and Mr Rochester's other guests suggest that Jane Eyre doesn't know her place either. She is always polite – Mr Rochester is her employer – but the first person narrative gives us a graphic account of her rebellious thoughts. *Jane Eyre*, a novel by a woman who had to publish initially under a male pseudonym in order to be taken seriously, can be interpreted as a feminist text, as seen when Jane expresses her belief that she is Rochester's equal in everything except social class and status. 'I don't think, sir, you have a right to command me, merely because you are older than I, or because you have seen more of the world than I have – your claim to superiority depends on the use you have made of your time and experience,' she tells him.

Whereas Jane's powerful dialogue impresses both the reader and Rochester, however, when Mr Emerson champions his son and freely expresses – against middle-class social etiquette – his socialist, atheist views, his speech creates palpable tension between him and his audience. Forster invites the reader to compare the emotionally honest George, who goes to work, *takes care of his father and who brings out a passion in Lucy which she is herself unaware of, with Cecil Vyse, as possible husbands for his heroine.*

Examiner's commentary

This student:

▾ expresses her ideas clearly and accurately, showing good knowledge and understanding

▾ connects the speeches of Jane and Mr Emerson in order to build her argument

▾ creates good cohesion across paragraphs by connecting the stages of her argument

▾ makes the point that the novel might have been received differently over a century ago when it was first written.

If the rest of this essay reached this level of performance, it is likely this student would be on course to achieve a notional grade A.

Step 2: Developing and linking: go with the flow

An essay is a very specific type of formal writing that requires an appropriate discourse structure. In the main body of your writing, you need to thread your developing argument through each paragraph consistently and logically, referring back to the terms established by the question itself, rephrasing and reframing as you go. It can be challenging to sustain the flow of your essay and keep firmly on track, but here are some techniques to help you:

▾ Ensure your essay doesn't disintegrate into a series of disconnected building blocks by creating a neat and stable bridge between one paragraph and the next.

▾ Use discourse markers – linking words and phrases like 'on the other hand', 'however', 'although' and 'moreover' – to hold the individual paragraphs of your essay together and signpost the connections between different sections of your overarching argument.

▾ Having set out an idea in Paragraph A, in Paragraph B you might need then to support it by providing a further example; if so, signal this to the reader with a statement such as *'Moreover Forster presents Mr Eager's Italian resembling "nothing so much as an acid whistling fountain" to reinforce the difference between his chilly unfeeling anger and the warm, harmless affection between the cab driver and his "Persephone".'*

▾ To change direction and challenge an idea begun in Paragraph A by acknowledging that it is open to interpretation, you could begin Paragraph

B with something like '***On the other hand***, *this view of the novel could be challenged by a feminist critic…*'

❚ Another typical paragraph-to-paragraph link is when you want to show that the original idea doesn't give the full picture. Here you could modify your original point with something like '*Although it is possible to see Mr Eager's remarks to the cab driver as snobbish and even racist, this view does not take account of the social context of the early 1900s when his comments would have seemed much less offensive to many English tourists in Italy.*'

Step 3: Concluding: seal the deal

In bringing your writing to a close you need to capture and clarify your response to the given view and make a relatively swift and elegant exit. Keep your final paragraph short and sweet. Now is not the time to introduce any new points but equally don't just reword everything you have already said either. Neat potential closers include:

❚ looping the last paragraph back to something you mentioned in your introduction to suggest that you have now said all that you have to say on the subject

❚ reflecting on your key points to reach a balanced overview

❚ ending with a punchy quotation that leaves the reader thinking

❚ discussing the contextual implications of the topic you have debated

❚ reversing expectations to end on an interesting alternative view

❚ stating why you think the main issue, theme or character under discussion is so central to the novel

❚ mentioning how different audiences over time might have responded to the topic you have been debating.

Student C

This student is concluding a comparative essay on *A Room with a View* and *Persuasion* as part of an AQA A exam-style A-level response.

Compare how the authors of two texts you have studied present ideas about love and social class.

Overall, and in conclusion, it is so true that both these books present the tensions between love and social class but that love matters more. I think this is shown very well in the part when Lucy tells Cecil she doesn't want to marry him after all. Forster means that Lucy now loves George but he doesn't say so in so many words. Cecil is quite upset and Forster says 'nothing became in love like the leaving of it' which is a quote from Shakespeare's Macbeth. Anne Elliot, on the other hand, is going back to an old relationship with a man, her mentor, Lady

Russell, persuaded her wasn't good enough for her. Anne's father thinks too much of himself and wanted Anne to do better in marriage.

Throughout the book, A Room with a View Lucy has been struggling with her feelings because deep down she fancies George, but he's not the right social class and she's been brought up to think that she would marry a different sort of man. At the end she marries George and they go back to Florence together where they first met – although in one of the films of the novel George then dies in World War I and Lucy goes back again later by herself. Forster makes George's father seem quite a rough sort of man although he's very fond of his son and wants him to marry Lucy because he can see they love each other. He uses a lot of irony like Jane Austen did to talk about social class and love. I agree overall that in A Room with a View love matters more than social class.

Examiner's commentary

This student:

- throws his points down in a rather haphazard way
- fails to finish by clarifying his argument or actively debating the original Task focus
- labels the technical term 'irony' but fails to identify a single clear example of the technique as used by Forster, let alone analyse its effects
- identifies the source of the *Macbeth* quote used in *Persuasion* without analysing its meaning in relation to the novel
- uses language which is sometimes inappropriately informal ('fancies', 'thinks too much of himself').

If the rest of this essay reached this level of performance, it is likely this student would be on course to achieve a notional grade C.

Building skills 2: Analysing texts in detail

Having discussed structuring your writing in the previous section, this section of the guide contains two more extracts from students' responses to *A Room with a View*. The next few pages will enable you to assess the extent to which these students have successfully demonstrated their writing skills and mastery of the Assessment Objectives to provide you with an index by which to measure the progress of your own skills. Both extracts come with a commentary to help you to identify what each student is doing well and/or what changes they would need to make in order to aim for a higher grade.

The main focus here is on the ways in which you can successfully include within your own well-structured writing clear and appropriate references both to *A Room with a View* and to the ways in which other readers have responded to the novel. In an examination, of course, the 'other reading' you need to refer to is encoded within the question itself: the 'given view' in other words. In a non-examined assessment unit, you will have more choice about which interpretation of the text you want to work with – but since you have much more time and may well have written your own question title, you have even less excuse to wander off the Task.

Student D

This student is writing an AQA A AS-level-style essay that compares *A Room with a View* with a collection of love poems, although the section that follows focuses solely upon the novel.

'Obstacles to happiness dominate the literature of love.' How far does this statement apply to two texts you have studied?

By far the greatest obstacle to Lucy's happiness is herself, in my opinion. At the beginning of the novel she is presented as having the potential to be strong and overcome the class barrier that separates her from George Emerson, however it takes Forster's central protagonist a long time to develop the confidence to defy convention. Writing during the Suffragette era and experimenting with new ways of writing (the explicit references to physical attraction, the ironic 'looking in' and commenting on characters, for instance), Forster presents Lucy as beginning to question her position as a young middle-class woman. She loses herself in the music of the passionate Romantic composer Beethoven, wanders into Florence alone and witnesses a murder, but is hampered by the fact that nothing in her background has conditioned her to think for herself about how to overcome the obstacles to happiness that she faces. This dichotomy dominates her relationships with Cecil Vyse and George Emerson. The former plans to teach her what to think, thus posing an obstacle to Lucy's future happiness, whereas the latter declares 'I want you to have your own thoughts even when I hold you in my arms.' Until the point at which mentally strong but now physically quite weak Mr Emerson finally persuades her to clear the 'muddle' and 'darkness' from her mind and admit the truth about her feelings for George, Lucy is presented as hiding in self-delusion and denial and thus blocking off her own route to happiness. It's a transition which takes place over the year of the novel's chronological trajectory and isn't complete until we see Lucy back in Florence as a mature, confident strong woman on her honeymoon at the end of the novel. From a feminist perspective Lucy has, within a few months, thrown off the shackles of the patriarchy and become George's equal, surmounting all the obstacles to love that lay across her path.

In contrast the refreshingly enlightened views which Forster presents in Mr Emerson are effectively a strong fixed point in the novel against which other characters can be measured. George and Cecil, and even Charlotte change. Mrs Honeychurch and Mr Beebe do not. Mr Emerson is adamantly both atheist and socialist, refusing to have his only son baptised in 'superstition and ignorance' and forthright about the Santa Croce 'workmen who weren't paid properly'. And these are long-held beliefs. His manners, with their lack of deference, annoy people and he, like George and Mr Beebe, is aware of it but he remains strong despite what is said about him although he is sympathetically presented as not wanting to upset others. He is, I would argue, presented as more consistently strong than Lucy.

Examiner's commentary

This student:

- ◥ creates a coherent argument with clear links between paragraphs (AO1)
- ◥ confidently embeds quotations within the syntax of her own sentences so that the flow of her writing is not interrupted (AO1, AO2)
- ◥ quotes frequently and relevantly – just a well-chosen word or two being enough at times (AO1, AO2)
- ◥ recognises that this question is about the presentation of obstacles to happiness in the literature of love and focuses on that in detail (AO1)
- ◥ mentions E.M. Forster as the maker of textual meaning frequently when analysing his methods and themes (AO2)
- ◥ refers to the feminist contexts of the novel. (AO3)

If the rest of this response reached this level of performance it is likely that this student would be on course to achieve a notional grade A.

Student E

Like Student D, this student is writing an AQA A AS-level-style essay that compares *A Room with a View* with a collection of love poems, although the section that follows focuses solely upon the novel.

'Obstacles to happiness dominate the literature of love.'

How far does this statement apply to two texts you have studied?

Lucy marries George although he is a lower social class than her so she does overcome the main obstacle to her happiness. Mr Eager sneers at the Emersons as 'working people' and Cecil who has no profession would have been a more suitable choice because his background is middle class although he's very controlling and Lucy decides in the end that he is 'intolerable'. And her mother is thankful when she jilts him although Mrs Honeychurch doesn't approve of the marriage to George either – Forster tells us that through a letter to Lucy from Freddy at the end of the novel when she's on her honeymoon in 'the room with a view'. Mr Beebe doesn't like the marriage either although he doesn't really like marriage much at all and Mr Eager hates the Emersons. So Lucy goes against the views of nearly everyone around her to marry George. Mr Emerson is the only person who supports her but he is regarded, by most, as not worth listening to because he's a socialist and an atheist. The reader obviously wants Lucy to marry someone who will respect her as an equal regardless of the class barrier and it's the main storyline in A Room with a View.

Examiner's commentary

This student:

- ▼ clearly knows the text well and uses brief direct quotations (AO1)
- ▼ shows awareness of Forster's narrative methods in referring to the letter from Freddy (AO2)
- ▼ makes no reference to the contexts in which the text was written or is read
- ▼ makes unsubstantiated sweeping statements such as Mr Beebe 'doesn't really like marriage much at all' and 'Mr Eager hates the Emersons'
- ▼ does not show sufficient awareness of Forster's role as text creator
- ▼ misses opportunities to signal awareness of possible alternative interpretations.

If the rest of this response reached this level of performance it is likely that this student would be on course to achieve a notional low grade C.

Extended commentaries

These three commentaries give close detailed analysis of key points in *A Room with a View*. They are not intended to reflect examination essays.

Lucy's music (Chapter 3, p.30)

Forster sets the scene for a two-paragraph omniscient authorial discussion about Lucy's relationship with music with the words 'It so happened' – a clause borrowed from fairy tales – to suggest something otherworldly. Anyone who can play music (and contextually this is before the era of mass recorded music so this is the only way a 'commonplace person' can experience it) can 'shoot into the empyrean' while listeners who are left behind marvel. Forster reinforces a sense of high-flown escape with the Greek word 'empyrean' the highest part of heaven, believed by the ancients to be a realm of pure fire.

Forster uses language from the semantic field of religion with words such as 'worship', 'visions' and 'empyrean' to underline the idea that music is for some a spiritual experience. At the same time music, like religion, is a social equaliser which 'will accept those whom breeding and intellect and culture have alike rejected'. And when Lucy plays she is 'no longer either' (a phrase Forster repeats rhetorically for emphasis) confined to a fixed role as she is in everyday life.

Interpreting music is a form of descriptive expression and in Lucy's playing, Forster's narrative voice observes, can be found 'all the furniture of the pictorial style'. Both 'furniture' and 'pictorial' suggest a comparison with humdrum domesticity. The language of formal musical criticism in the second paragraph deals with Lucy's unremarkable technique 'no dazzling *exécutante*' (the rather pretentious French word for 'player'). She has learned the piano, by inference, because that's what middle-class young ladies are expected to do, and gets 'no more right notes than was suitable for one of her age and situation'. Forster's witty use of the negative here suggests Lucy doesn't play particularly well but that she does so with feeling and emotion that moves her listeners. 'Passion was there', Forster says, reversing conventional subject and verb syntax to stress the word 'passion'.

Forster's use of the first person plural pronouns 'we' and 'us' here flatters the reader as part of an assertion that the reader, like the novelist, will understand without further explanation 'that some sonatas of Beethoven are written tragic no one can gainsay'.

Mr Eager on the Emersons (Chapter 5, pp.54/6)

This passage consists of dialogue between Mr Eager and Lucy with interjections from Charlotte. Forster breaks into the conversation without introduction as Mr Eager, using the sort of denigrating language which might outrage a Marxist critic, percussively dismisses Mr Emerson as the 'son of a labourer' and a 'mechanic of some sort' who later took to 'writing for the socialistic press'. The narrative voice then confirms what the reader has probably already deduced: 'They were talking about the Emersons.'

Forster then has Mr Eager use the strangely inappropriately grudging word 'sympathy' to explain his usual feelings about 'working people' and their 'desire for education and social advance'. It is loaded with feelings of sorrow and regret. 'Admiration' is beyond Forster's unpleasant chaplain. Mr Eager's careful use of the negative 'not wholly vile' is telling too. By inference Forster seems to be suggesting that for Mr Eager, the Emersons *are* wholly vile.

Mr Eager then hints that there is something important about the Emersons which Lucy and Charlotte don't know. And so venomous does Forster, apparently, want to make this character that his threat to expose the Emersons is 'hissed'. Challenged by Lucy, openly objecting 'for the first time in her life', Mr Eager, determined to save his own face, blurts out the dramatic 'That man murdered his wife.' It is repeated twice more and toned down each time until it becomes 'That man has murdered his wife in the face of God.' Lucy meanwhile remains initially calm (and Charlotte is silent). Her first question is simply 'How?' although a few lines later she is 'losing her courage' and trying to distance herself or 'relapsing into the old chaotic methods' as Forster has it.

Mr Eager is presented as self-absorbed, vain and effectively untruthful here. He proceeds with his accusations largely because 'It was intolerable that she should disbelieve him.' He demands of Lucy to know whether the Emersons said anything against him to her while they were all at Santa Croce and comments 'Oh, I thought they had been libelling me to you.' Like 'murder', 'libel' is a strong word from the semantic field of the law and Forster makes it clear that Mr Eager is twisting the truth for his own purposes. He also sneers at Lucy for succumbing to the 'personal charms' of the Emersons which has led to her wish to 'defend them'. The irony here is that Mr Eager is actually right. Lucy *is* affected by the charms of the Emersons although it will be a long time before she understands that.

George's declaration (Chapter 16, p.174)

At this pivotal moment in the novel Forster gives us George, hitherto usually a man of few words, pouring out his thoughts articulately in one continuous paragraph to Lucy and it's one of the longest speeches in *A Room with a View*. His language is blunt and his sentences are often short. 'I would never have let myself go', 'I'm not ashamed' and 'I don't apologise'. He uses everyday language and many monosyllables such as 'things', 'sort', 'joy' and 'daren't'. It is entirely free from the complex Latin- or Greek-derived vocabulary and classical allusions which pepper Cecil's pretentious speech. Some of the sentences are conventionally ungrammatical ('Cecil all over again') to convey rapid, even angry speech. Together these devices have the effect of making the tone both urgent and serious.

George's speech moves rapidly from one topic to another because he is so impassioned. Condemnatory of 'your Cecil' to whom Lucy is still engaged at this point, he goes on to criticise Cecil, who 'daren't let a woman decide', for trying to shape Lucy as he wants her to be rather than, by implication, admiring and loving her for what she already is. He has observed Cecil guiding Lucy with regard to 'what's charming, amusing or ladylike' or even 'womanly' — all adjectives suggestive of the sort of polite, narrow, middle-class life Lucy has been brought up to. Men like Cecil, George declares hyperbolically but simply, have 'kept Europe back for a thousand years'. He is enraged by having to watch Lucy acquiesce to all this domineering. Forster presents him expressing his frustration both at the rectory and at Windy Corner with the words '…you, you of all women listen to his voice instead of your own'. The emphatic repetition of the word 'you' stresses George's conviction that Lucy has unusual individual qualities and her own mind.

Then, in a rather oblique way ('and you may not have noticed…'), he declares his love and the reasons for his decision to speak out against Cecil: 'therefore I settled to fight him'. George has kissed Lucy twice suddenly and without overt encouragement, which some critics have interpreted as symbolic loss of virginity. Here he cautiously laments his lack of self-control but says baldy and boldly in two very short sentences, both of which confound what Lucy might be expecting by inserting a negative: 'I'm not ashamed. I don't apologise.'

▲ Rafe Spall as George in the 2007 film

Before studying this section you should identify your own 'top ten quotations' – i.e. those phrases or sentences that seem to encapsulate a key theme or aspect of the text most aptly and memorably – and clearly work out what it is about your choices that make each one so significant. No two readers of *A Room with a View* will select exactly the same set and it is worth discussing them with – and perhaps having to defend them to – fellow students.

Then look carefully at the list below and consider each one's significance in interpretation of the novel. How might you use them to support your explorations or readings of *A Room with a View*? What do these quotations indicate about Forster's ideas, themes and methods and the various potential ways in which the text can be interpreted?

1

The kind old man who had allowed her to see the lights dancing in the Arno, and the cypresses of San Miniato, and the foothills of the Apennines, black against the rising moon. (p.14)

> This grateful response to Mr Emerson is posited from Lucy's point of view although the voice is the narrator's. It is significant because at one level it simply means that she is pleased to have the titular room with a view she's been promised. It is also symbolic. On arrival in Florence Lucy's view of the world is very limited. While there she learns a great deal about life as well as the rather narrow, circumscribed education about paintings and buildings she seeks. This reference to Mr Emerson's kindness prefigures what he will teach her much later – that she has to let her background and its fixed teaching go in order to be able to live life fully in her love for George. Literally she can see lights, trees and dark unknown hills in the distance. These could be taken to represent the excitement of love, the stability of a solid relationship and the distant unknowns which lay in her future. This quotation illustrates how Mr Emerson differs from every other adult in Lucy's life and the influence he is to have on her.

'Built by faith indeed! That simply means that the workmen weren't paid properly.' (Mr Emerson to Lucy, p.24)

2

⊿ Mr Emerson is a socialist. He champions working people and disapproves of their being exploited by people who have inherited their money and do not work for their living. This way of thinking is so far from Lucy's own milieu, and regarded as a threat by many in her social class, that she considers this and his atheism as curiously exotic. She suspects that her mother might 'not like her talking to that kind of person' and knows that Charlotte 'would object most strongly'. Mr Emerson's socialism is part of the social class theme of the novel and comes through several times later. This quotation is the first time that his politics are made clear to the reader as well as to Lucy. As such, it would be a useful quotation if you were commenting from a socialist or Marxist critical perspective. It also exemplifies an aspect of Forster's presentation of social class.

he was trustworthy, intelligent and even kind; he might even have had a high opinion of her. But he lacked chivalry; his thoughts, like his behaviour, would not be modified by awe. (p.46)

3

⊿ This summary of George Emerson's character comes fairly early in the novel when Lucy has met him only recently and just after he has removed her from the murder she has witnessed. Forster makes it clear that George, like his father is truthful, reliable and respectful but he will not defer to, or be intimidated by Lucy and her circle simply because he is of a different social class. The straightforwardness and lack of class-driven **obfuscation** is stressed almost every time he and Lucy are together. Even at the end of the novel after they're married, Forster comments that George 'dislikes any darkness' (p.219) by which he means confusion, misunderstanding or 'muddle'.

obfuscation: never saying what you really think; dressing it up as something else.

'But it is such an awkward size. It is too large for the peasant class and too small for anyone in the least like ourselves.' (p.107)

4

⊿ Landlord Sir Harry Otway describes to Mrs Honeychurch, Lucy and Cecil the difficulties of finding tenants to rent Cissie Villa opposite the church in the centre of the village. This is the house eventually occupied by the Emersons at Cecil's 'humorous' instigation. It illustrates the social class divide which permeates English society in 1908. None of the characters present can conceive of people like the Emersons for whom the house will be ideal – they're literate, intelligent, courteous people and certainly not peasants, but neither are they landed gentry. This section of society grew rapidly in the nineteenth and early twentieth centuries and hundreds of thousands of houses like Cissie Villa were built between around 1890 and the outbreak of war in 1914 to house them. Every town in the country still has some of them.

5 A Radical out and out, she learned to speak with horror of Suburbia. Life as far as she troubled to conceive it, was a circle of rich, pleasant people with identical interests and identical foes. In this circle one thought, married and died. Outside it were poverty and vulgarity. (pp.114–15)

> This neat summary of Lucy's state of mind encapsulates the prevailing attitude among the Honeychurch social circle. It doesn't describe a Radical at all. The outlook is deeply conservative. When she agrees to marry Cecil, Lucy is at a pivotal point in her life. A life with Cecil would mean exactly the society she has grown up in. Because she yearns – she isn't fully aware of the yearning but Mr Beebe can hear it in her Beethoven – to be a fully developed independent human being rather than an inferior appendage to a man, she will eventually turn her back on everything described in this quotation. When we see her with George in Florence at the end of the novel her only contact with home is letters from the ever-affable Freddy.

6 How dreadful if she [Lucy] really wished to remain near him [George]! Of course, the wish was due to nerves, which love to play such perverse tricks on us. (p.148)

> This is the perfect example of Forster commenting on Lucy's state of mind and her attempts to deny the truth of what she is really feeling. Her upbringing and conditioning tell her that George is unsuitable and yet something inexplicable is happening. She wants very much to be near George. The reader can see exactly what's happening. It is only Lucy who cannot so it is also a useful illustration of Forster's irony.

7 more of her defences fell and she entertained an image that had physical beauty… (p.149)

> Lucy has met George in Surrey, chatted to him while flanked by Cecil and convinced herself that all is well. She believes that 'She loved Cecil' but acknowledges that 'George made her nervous' (p.148). As she relaxes into self-delusion she begins to think, in spite or herself, about how attractive George's appearance is. Forster is taking the reader step by step subtly through the sexual awakening which George is gradually triggering in Lucy.

He [Cecil] could not know that this was the most intimate conversation they had ever had. (p.213)

8

> ◥ This line underscores the distance that exists between Cecil and Lucy. He has just tried to kiss her in a wood, an attempt even he has to acknowledge has 'been a failure'. He is regretting his inability to be spontaneous when Lucy suddenly tells him Mr Emerson's real name because she's ashamed of her pointless lie earlier. Because Lucy has inexplicable feelings about George and his kiss, telling Cecil the real name is a declaration of trust or a resolve to be more truthful. But it's not exactly an intimacy as this ironic comment stresses. There is also a plot device here. If Cecil had not known the Emersons' name he would not have been able to capitalise on the chance meeting at the National Gallery which is what brings George to Summer Street.

'You love the boy body and soul, plainly, directly, as he loves you, and no other word expresses it.' (p.212)

9

> ◥ The significance of Mr Emerson's statement lies partly in its desperate simplicity and directness. Lucy loves George – but she has been in what a modern reader would call 'denial' since he looked after her in Florence following the violent street murder in Chapter 4. Now, at last, with Lucy just about to depart to Greece with the Miss Alans, she hears and accepts the truth because Mr Emerson expresses it so unequivocally. It summarises the heart of the novel's message and is its ultimate turning point. Lucy heeds Mr Emerson and sees her future clearly. Forster doesn't bother with the details of the months which follow; the next time we meet Lucy she is back at the Pension Bertolini – enjoying A Room with a View of a rich future as George's wife as well as of the River Arno outside her window.

He [Mr Emerson] had robbed the body of its taint, the world's taunts of their sting; he had shown her [Lucy] the holiness of direct desire. (p.215)

10

> ◥ This triumphant authorial declaration makes it clear that the generous humanist philosophy of Mr Emerson has at last got through to Lucy. No longer is she so hidebound by convention that she has to 'lie' to everyone – including herself – about her love and, specifically, her sexual desire for George. Finally the novel's heroine is ready to emerge from her chrysalis and blossom like a butterfly into a new and modern woman capable of making up her own mind and following the dictates of her own heart rather than the strictures of her narrow-minded social class.

Books

Other novels (various editions) by E.M. Forster which may offer common themes or comparable ideas include:

- *Where Angels Fear to Tread* (1905)
- *Howard's End* (1910)
- *A Passage to India* (1924)

See also E.M. Forster's 1927 book *Aspects of the Novel* (Penguin Classics), an account of his Clark lectures at Trinity College Cambridge in which he, quite entertainingly, sets down his ideas about novels and how they work.

Concerning E.M. Forster by Frank Kermode (Weidenfeld and Nicholson, 2009) is a very authoritative reassessment of Forster's work which examines the reasons for his century-long popularity when many other Edwardian novelists have gone out of fashion.

Arctic Summer by Damon Galgut (Atlantic Books, 2014) is a fictional re-imagining of Forster's life which includes interesting, if speculative, insights.

E.M. Forster: A Life by P.N. Furbank (Secker and Warburg, 1979) is a biography which includes critical and contextual comment on Forster's work.

E.M. Forster: A Literary Life by Mary Iago (Macmillan, 1995) is a more recent biography with further insights.

Cambridge Companion to E.M. Forster edited by David Bradshaw (CUP, 2007) is a useful and eclectic collection of information and critical responses from the publication of Forster's earliest work through to the twenty-first century.

E.M. Forster edited by Jeremy Tambling (Macmillan – New Casebooks, 1995) is a collection of scholarly critical essays. The opening essay 'Forster's Trespasses: Tourism and Cultural Politics' by James Buzard is particularly relevant to *A Room with a View*.

The Edwardian Turn of Mind: The First World War and English Culture by Samuel Hynes (Pimlico, 1992) was first published in 1955. It's a fascinating and rewarding read and fills in the contextual background of *A Room with a View* brilliantly.

E.M. Forster by Claude J. Summers (Frederick Ungar, 1983, First English Edition 1984). Gay, American academic and critic, Summers is strong on Forster's homosexuality and how it affects his writing.

Articles

'Love, Actually' by Zadie Smith, *Guardian*, 1 November 2003. Smith, an acclaimed novelist herself, is a great Forster admirer and champion. Here she explains why. Accessed February 2016 at: www.theguardian.com/books/2003/nov/01/classics.zadiesmith

'Fiction and E.M. Forster' by Frank Kermode, *London Review of Books*, 10 May 2007. Distillation of some of the ideas which were to appear in Kermode's book two years later.

Films

James Ivory's 1985 version is reasonably true to the novel and Helena Bonham-Carter gets the essence of Lucy. Maggie Smith's performance as Charlotte is excellent, and Simon Callow and Judi Dench are very well cast as Mr Beebe and Miss Lavish.

The 2007 film directed by Nicholas Renton uses a screenplay by Andrew Davies and imposes a World War I framing device which distances it from the novel. Worth seeing, though, for father and son Timothy and Rafe Spall as the Emersons and for Laurence Fox's impressive interpretation of Cecil.